TRACING THE ESSAY

THROUGH EXPERIENCE TO TRUTH

TRACING THE ESSAY

THROUGH EXPERIENCE TO TRUTH

G. DOUGLAS ATKINS

THE UNIVERSITY OF GEORGIA PRESS
Athens and London

© 2005 by The University of Georgia Press
Athens, Georgia 30602
www.ugapress.org
All rights reserved

Designed by Emily Cavett Taff
Set in 11.5 on 15 by BookComp, Inc.

Most University of Georgia Press Books are
available from popular e-book vendors.

Printed digitally

Library of Congress Cataloging-in-Publication Data
Atkins, G. Douglas (George Douglas), 1943–
Tracing the essay : through experience to truth / G. Douglas Atkins.
ix, 180 p. ; 22 cm.
Includes bibliographical references (p. 163–171) and index.
ISBN-10: 0-8203-2761-1 (hardcover : alk. paper)
ISBN-10: 0-8203-2787-5 (pbk. : alk. paper)
ISBN-13: 978-0-8203-2761-7 (hardcover : alk. paper)
ISBN-13: 978-0-8203-2787-7 (pbk. : alk. paper)
1. Essay. I. Title.
PN4500.A895 2005
809.4—dc22
2005017466

British Library Cataloging-in-Publication Data available

To the memory of my mother and my father.

To the memory of my mother and my father

CONTENTS

ix
Preface

1
Introduction

9
Irony or Sneakiness
On the Essay's Second-Class Citizenship

27
Home-Cosmography
The Renaissance Basis of the Essay

47
The Most Self-Centered of Forms?
Distinguishing the Essay

63
Assaying Experience
Time, Meaning, and the Essay

95
Paradox Abounding
Tension and the Via Media *Nature of the Essay*

123
Form and Meaning
The Essay's Immanent Purposiveness

145
In-Betweenness
The Burden of the Essay

163
Notes

173
Index

PREFACE

In *Estranging the Familiar* (Georgia, 1992), I embraced "the return of/to the essay" and explored its value for literary criticism. Here, I probe more deeply and widely, hoping to interest a larger audience. There, I ended with an essay—or at least a memoir—about my parents, now deceased and much missed, both of them. I dedicate this book to their memory and in gratitude for their sacrifices, many and great, and for the joys of our last years together, South Carolinians transplanted in Kansas. T. S. Eliot prays, at the end of *Ash-Wednesday*, "not to be separated." I was not, at last, and am not, separated from them. The essay, I now surmise, functions as one agent of the holy tension that works against separation.

With pleasure and humility I acknowledge other debts: to the enormously helpful and supportive readers for the Press, Scott Russell Sanders and Lynn Worsham, who bear no responsibility for any remaining errors, lapses, and infelicities; to the equally helpful, supportive, and always affable staff at the Press, especially Nancy Grayson, to whom I am also much indebted, and Jennifer Reichlin and Gay Gragson; to Lori Whitten, once again, for typing with consummate skill and amazing good cheer; to my children, again, Leslie, now a professor (of theatre), an author, and a new mother, and Christopher, already expert in early European art history, married, and finishing up his dissertation; and to my wife Rebecca, whose heart is big enough to accommodate and to humanize my head—together we associate sensibility, I reckon. Thank you, all!

TRACING THE ESSAY

THROUGH EXPERIENCE TO TRUTH

INTRODUCTION

MY LIFE CHANGED the day I rediscovered the essay. In freshman English twenty-five years before, we had been forced to read essays and then to attempt a few of our own. I hated reading J. B. Priestley and Francis Bacon and Oliver Wendell Holmes and failed miserably at trying to write like them. I shamelessly hated even more my instructor, who admired Lionel Trilling, adored and imitated Scott Fitzgerald, and found my admittedly inchoate writing repulsive. Happily, or so I then thought, after escaping with an "A" thanks to acing a grammar exam, I had no more to do with essays in college or in graduate school: we read none, and we wrote "articles," scholarly, impersonal, important. Not until the mid-1980s did I encounter Edward Hoagland, Richard Selzer, Nancy Mairs, Hilaire Belloc, and Cynthia Ozick and make a responsible effort to cope with this "formless form." When I discovered these essayists, my life, both professional and personal, changed.[1]

The exact day of my discovery I do not now recall, nor does it much matter. My discovery had to do with sentences, those building blocks or "pack mules" I had never much considered.[2] I was still far from a style that Ozick celebrates and incarnates as "comely and muscular," but I began to admire the craft apparent in Hoagland and the rhetorical mastery of Dr. Selzer. Working on sentences, too, helped to close the gap between my father and me: he could neither read nor write, but as a mechanic he could make an engine purr, his work as comely in its way as it was muscular. Maybe, I began to imagine, I could make sentences run the way his cars did, smoothly and efficiently.

I say my life then changed professionally because I began to teach the essay as an art form, which is quite a different approach from how I was taught in college. In my literature courses I was asking students to make essays themselves, not in emulation of those we read, but rather in response to them and, more important, as an attempt—an *essai*—to draw meaning from their personal experience. To my surprise, I soon found myself offering a course in essay writing. This essay course is part of our creative-writing curriculum, which I had once regarded as a weak link and of which I could not have imagined myself a part. As I taught the history, the tradition, and the making of essays, I found my way of teaching changing. Workshops form the staple of creative-writing courses. Contrary to my prejudicial opinion of them, I discovered they are neither a waste of students' time nor an easy way for one to fill an hour (with very little outside preparation). Instead, they are a way to improve student writing by giving them an audience, providing response from several quarters and perspectives, and allowing them to follow up with questions concerning strategies, effectiveness, and reception of meaning. In addition, it soon became clear that I was still teaching literature, and in more than one way. We always begin with roughly a month of reading "classic" instances of the form: Montaigne, Bacon, Johnson, Hazlitt, Belloc, Eliot, Woolf, Orwell, White, and usually, time permitting, two or three others. But the students' own essays I began to treat as literature too, or at least as an attempt to make literature. A work is not an essay if it isn't both personal and artful, I insist. You can't write, or at least don't write, with fullness of texture and sense of technique and form if you don't read, I also insist. So I wind up teaching writing and reading together, which is the way it should be in all English courses. As Geoffrey Hartman has put it, the difference reading most often makes is writing, writing being a response to reading. Reading is often a propaedeutic to writing just as writing produces the need and the very reason for reading. You chance upon Selzer's sentences, or Ozick's, as upon Sir Thomas Browne's and, differently, Dr. Johnson's, and you realize some of the wonders of language and the art that sentences alone make. I wanted to read more of their kind and to try my hand at this supple but stubborn and insistent medium that, in resisting, strengthens me.

I soon found myself writing about the essay, and as someone has well reasoned, you can't write about essays in article form—inevitably you wind up writing an essay. And I did. Most of my writing of essays has been of the critical sort. Once or twice I veered off into personal, actually autobiographical, writing closer to the memoir, but I soon recognized that my strength, if any, lies elsewhere, although I still hope someday to write something akin to Woolf's "On Being Ill" and Sam Pickering's "Composing a Life." That said, it would have been astounding had I not changed—developed—personally as a result of my deep and abiding professional engagement with the essay. I certainly cannot credit a literary form for making me a better, more compassionate and capacious person—although I do believe I am that. However, I am convinced that the essay did contribute to the direction my private life has taken, enforcing certain (new) tendencies, obviating others, guiding me with a gentle but also admonitory hand toward "envisioning the stranger's heart" (a pregnant phrase I take from the great stylist Cynthia Ozick). Teaching the essay, celebrating it, and, in fact, preaching it, I work daily where the mean-spirited hold no sway, where openness and receptivity drive response and determine action, where poise, balance, respect, and a host of traditional virtues shake the dust from their clothes and boots and saunter forth with eyes wide open. Humility is perhaps the chief of these other virtues, foundation sufficient indeed for the essay.

No essayist is a perfect human being; all of us fail, to more or less degree, to embody the essayistic virtues—which brings us back around to the chicken-or-the-egg question, on which I direct considerable attention. To what degree, or extent, *is* the essay responsible for the formation of character, that character so attractive and without which we are apt to quit reading? I suspect, although I can hardly prove it, that most essayists *are* good people. Claiming that candor is "the basic ingredient" of the form, E. B. White says that if you try to fake it, you'll soon be found out, and I expect he's right in that as in so much else.

I expect to write elsewhere of an "essayistic teaching," and I seek in my teaching to embody as many of the essay's virtues as I am capable of. The risk, the unsympathetic rightly point out, is that the classroom may become Oprah-ized, become merely a place of empowerment and enhanced self-esteem where students come to "feel better about themselves" as they pursue a writing admittedly liberating as well as personal. Freed from the shackles of the five-paragraph form, the necessity of a thesis statement at the end of the opening paragraph, and the logical demands of the (prized) article that they are making whether they know it or not, students may, initially, suppose that "anything goes." But freedom entails responsibility and never quite equates with license, and the essay is a form, no matter how evanescent or difficult to describe. What the essay teaches the teacher is not just openness but also an antidogmatism related to its historical skepticism—and there is nothing, in my experience, that the academy needs more than a healthy dose of humility. You can't fully embrace the essay without subscribing to its principles, adopting them, and putting them into practice. It thus turns out that the essay is a very demanding form.

Some, myself among them, have written of the essay's "spirit." What they, for example Thomas Harrison in *Essayism*,[3] mean by this is that the virtues associated with the essay transcend the form, as if floating above it, able and even likely to fall in unsuspected places, like the novel. While in some ways attractive and tempting, this argument represents, as stated in the late Marxist Georg Lukács's *Soul and Form*, a perversion of understanding that goes by the name of "incarnation." We reach, here, the heart of my argument concerning the essay as "embodied truth," the intersection of experience and meaning, idea and form (or body). There is no avoiding religious questions in dealing with this famously skeptical form, in which issues of immanence and transcendence loom large and require close attention.

I have much to say about these matters in the pages ahead. They link up, as it happens, with autobiographical concerns. What the essay has done for me, I must insist, cannot be strained out and made into an ethereal spirit. The essay remains, on the contrary, stubbornly literal and material—although it is not merely that. The essay's form is essential, also the most difficult aspect of the essay to write about. Thus it is that many authors before me have floundered on the shoals of a distinction between the personal essay and the familiar essay, which I shall consider at length later on. I understand and sympathize, therefore, with those who resign themselves to the epithet "formless form."

INTRODUCTION

What the maker of essays experiences, at some point, has been wonderfully stated by Joseph Epstein, who, borrowing from the painter Paul Klee, titled a collection of his familiar essays *A Line Out for a Walk*. (You give yourself up to the direction of the writing, your will surrendered . . . and I have, without consciously setting out to do so, illustrated the point here.) In taking "a line out for a walk," essayists may seem destined for the terminus reached by the "enthusiastic" and mad hack writer who narrates *A Tale of a Tub*: "to write upon *Nothing*; when the subject is utterly exhausted, to let the pen still move on"[4] (appositely the essayist Hilaire Belloc published collections bearing the titles *On Nothing*, *On Something*, *On Anything*, and, simply, *On*). But, in fact, *the essayist writes about something*. He or she becomes the crucible in which experience is tried and tested and meaning extracted. The essay's subject is not, then, the self, contrary to popular opinion, although the essayist's soil, or laboratory, is nothing but the self.

Often—again, contrary to popular opinion among scholars—that "something" the essayist writes about is important rather than slight, trivial, inconsequential, and merely frivolous. Belloc's "The Mowing of a Field" is a perfect instance of essayistic manner and procedure: the mundane occasion opens an avenue for quite serious and significant cultural critique. How the essay, such as Belloc's, or his friend Chesterton's "A Piece of Chalk," or Virginia Woolf's "Death of the Moth," becomes something more than its title promises was suggested by Georg Lukács in a well-known essay nearly a century ago. In due course I shall take up Lukács's argument at length.

In this wonderful—the *Antioch Review* calls it "glorious"[5]—form, you talk about something by talking about yourself (although the obverse does not quite obtain: essayists don't characteristically talk about themselves by discussing "something"). Thus it is that essays frequently begin with the innocent-looking prepositions "on" or "of." Without intending to do so, I have illustrated this point too as I move back and forth between the personal and the professional differences essays have made in my life.

Truth to tell, in my experience the essay has become that sought-for though unexpected meeting-place and crossing-point of the professional and the personal. I have been, by turns, an eighteenth-century scholar, a theorist (or at least a commentator on and expositor of theory), and a specialist in the essay, one who both teaches and writes about the form and its history and also instructs in the creation of that form. I know now, with all necessary certainty, that my moves were neither happenstance nor perverse. My three "subfields" are interrelated, and as things have come together for me with the essay, there is an unmistakable sense of rightness. It's like falling in love and knowing that the person you love is the right one: you simply and surely know. I do not claim to have *associated* my sensibility—Eliot having argued that in the seventeenth century thinking and feeling became dissociated, an occurrence from which we had not, at least in his time, recovered; I do, however, both understand and share the narrator's sense in Flaubert's *Madame Bovary* that happiness consists of the union of temperament and circumstance. I will be happier still if, in the following pages, you, gentle reader, find the circumstances of the essay to be congenial to your temperament. Beware, though, for this slight thing has the power to modify that temperament.

IRONY OR SNEAKINESS
ON THE ESSAY'S SECOND-CLASS CITIZENSHIP

⁓

The essayist, unlike the novelist, the poet, and the playwright, must be content in his self-imposed role of second-class citizen. A writer who has his sights trained on the Nobel Prize or other earthly triumphs had best write a novel, a poem, or a play, and leave the essayist to ramble about, content with living a free life and enjoying the satisfactions of a somewhat undisciplined existence.
E. B. White, foreword, *Essays*

The essayist dismisses his own proud hopes which sometimes lead him to believe that he has come close to the ultimate: he has, after all, no more to offer than explanations of the poems of others, or at best of his own ideas. But he ironically adapts himself to this smallness—the eternal smallness of the most profound work of the intellect in the face of life—and even emphasizes it with ironic modesty.
Georg Lukács, "On the Nature and Form of the Essay"

⁓

THE ESSAY is, of course, the form literary commentary has traditionally taken, at least until the MLA, German scholarship, and so-called professionalism expunged *belles lettres* in favor of the book-length monograph and the "definite article," which are impersonal, closed, purely logical, and authoritarian. What we call "criticism" counts for little in the world outside academia: it sells more anemically than even poetry and is often to be found, if at all, in the farthest, darkest reaches of bookshops. If criticism offers no cachet to the essay, where to look for its significance?

And the essay *is* significant, having survived midcentury proclamations of its demise (delivered, sometimes, with strained irony), and having managed a recent comeback so widespread and vigorous that even textbooks now grant it canonical and genre status alongside poetry, fiction, and drama. Nothing short of a renaissance of the essay has been underway for at least two decades. Possessed, therefore, of remarkable resiliency, the essay has endured drought and doubt, exclusion from the pantheon of genres, and a lack of academic recognition. It has now blossomed, cultivated by writers and eagerly sought by admiring readers interested in "the real."

Perhaps one reason for the essay's impoverishing "second-class" citizenship, as E. B. White labeled it in 1977, lies in its characteristic modesty; refusing to "take on airs," the essay often appears so unassuming as to be self-effacing, which is certainly part of its charm as well as of its power. Its brevity—the essay can often be read in one sitting—militates against epic pretensions or visions of grandeur, before which the maker of essays is, besides, uncomfortable and wary. Accordingly, the essay has never flaunted itself the way the novel sometimes does; rather, it declares its importance through its difference from the romance, history, and biography. The essay has, typically, manifested contentment with itself, although just as typically it manifests discontentment with the world surrounding it.

FROM THE BEGINNING, indeed, modesty has characterized the essay. Lukács refers to "the wonderfully elegant and apt title of 'Essays'" Montaigne gave his mere trials or attempts as "simple modesty" and "an arrogant courtesy."[1] Arrogance is hard to find, but otherwise the Hungarian theorist is surely right. Modesty there is everywhere in Montaigne, along with elegance, nowhere more so than when he tries, simply, to defend his undertaking, an *apologia pro sua essais* that turns "Of Practice" from a personal account of a near-death experience into a seminal revelation of the essayist's art: "What I write here," offers the wily old Gascon, "is not my teaching, but my study; it is not a lesson for others, but for me." Both becoming and beguiling, "the father of the essay" continues, edging his defense a major step forward with the same humility:

> And yet it should not be held against me if I publish what I write. What is useful to me may also by accident be useful to another. Moreover, I am not spoiling anything, I am using only what is mine. And if I play the fool, it is at my expense and without harm to anyone. For it is a folly that will die with me, and will have no consequences. We have heard of only two or three ancients who opened up this road [presumably not including Seneca and

Plutarch, about whom Montaigne writes extensively in other *essais*], and even of them we cannot say whether their manner in the least resembled mine, since we know only their names. No one since has followed their lead. It is a thorny undertaking, and more so than it seems, to follow a movement so wandering as that of our mind, to penetrate the opaque depths of its innermost folds, to pick out and immobilize the innumerable flutterings that agitate it. And it is a new and extraordinary amusement, which withdraws us from the ordinary occupations of the world, yes, even from those most recommended.[2]

Only an "amusement," insists Montaigne, intended for himself—and yet the penultimate sentence here stands as perhaps the most forthright description ever of the essayist's wondrous mapping of the undulations of his own, simple, humble cogitations. At any rate, Montaigne proceeds, acutely aware of the novelty of his effort and the risk he runs in making the personal and the private public. His attempt is a major step, of not-unmitigated good, in the movement of Western mind and culture:

It is many years now that I have had only myself as object of my thoughts, that I have been examining and studying only myself; and if I study anything else, it is in order promptly to apply it to myself, or rather within myself. And it does not seem to me that I am making a mistake if—as is done in the other sciences, which are incomparably less useful—I impart what I have learned in this one, though I am hardly satisfied with the progress I have made in it. There is no description equal in difficulty, or certainly in usefulness, to the description of oneself. Even so one must spruce up, even so one must present oneself in an orderly arrangement, if one would go out in public. Now, I am constantly adorning myself, for I am constantly describing myself.³

A significant admission, this last, dispelling the notion that the essayist writes without craft, without concern for shape and form.

To that point, I will return in due course and at some length. For now, I move to the concluding paragraphs of the essay "Of Practice." Here, Montaigne confronts the major moral objection to his undertaking:

> It seems to [some] that to be occupied with oneself means to be pleased with oneself, that to frequent and associate with oneself means to cherish oneself too much. That may be. But this excess arises only in those who touch themselves no more than superficially; who observe themselves only after taking care of their business; who call it daydreaming and idleness to be concerned with oneself, and making castles in Spain to furnish and build oneself; who think themselves something alien and foreign to themselves.⁴

Whereas Montaigne's objectors would have it that writing about oneself—that is, essaying—breeds self-satisfaction and vanity, he claims the opposite, ending with paragraphs embodying the modesty that he everywhere embraces and showing the Ancient side of this Modern:

> If anyone gets intoxicated with his knowledge when he looks beneath him, let him turn his eyes upward toward past ages, and he will lower his horns, finding there so many thousands of minds that trample him underfoot. If he gets into some flattering presumption about his valor, let him remember the lives of the two Scipios, so many armies, so many nations, all of whom leave him so far behind

them. No particular quality will make a man proud who balances it against the many weaknesses and imperfections that are also in him, and, in the end, against the nullity of man's estate.

Because Socrates alone had seriously digested the precept of his god—to know himself—and because by that study he had come to despise himself, he alone was declared worthy of the name *wise*. Whoever knows himself thus, let him boldly make himself known by his own mouth.[5]

Of course, no man is without some pretension, vanity, and arrogance, and Montaigne's appears when he describes his essaying as "incomparably" more useful than "the other sciences." I find that rare slip—if that is what it is—less damaging than realistic and indicative of the tension that marks the essay as form. It does little or nothing to tarnish the picture that emerges of the essayist's modesty and humility.

The self-questioning—*que sais-je?*—that Montaigne bequeathed to the essay works against dogmatism and toward the modesty of which I have been speaking. In Montaigne's successors, that modesty assumes several forms and takes a number of guises. "A taste for littleness" marks the essay, said Abraham Cowley, writing in the seventeenth century in an essay titled "Of Greatness": "I confess I love littleness almost in all things. A little convenient estate, a little cheerful house, a little company, and a very little feast; and, if," he continues, "I were ever to fall in love again (which is a great passion, and therefore I hope I have done with it) it would be, I think, with prettiness, rather than with majestical beauty."[6] A taste for the sublime—or for the monumental—rarely affects the essayist. Believing that humility and penitence are "the foundation of the Christian religion,"[7] T. S. Eliot wrote of his friend, the sadly neglected Charles Whibley: "He was too modest, and had too varied tastes and interests in life, to care to be the monumental critic; and indeed, the monumental and encyclopedic critic is to be regarded with a carefully appraising eye; for the monument is sometimes constructed either by indifference to literature or by indifference to life."[8] Truth to tell, the essayist frequently runs up against, and admits to, his own vain hopes, inadequacies, and failures. Further tension thus marks the essay, for its makers "have occasionally had to wrestle with what might be called the stench of ego." After all, one "can write about himself from angles that are charmed, fond, delightfully nervy; alter the lens just a little and he crosses over into gloating, pettiness, defensiveness, score settling . . . or whining about his victimization. The trick is to realize that one is not important, except insofar as one's example can serve to elucidate a more widespread human trait and make readers feel a little less lonely and freakish."[9] Paradigmatically modest, Hilaire Belloc even denies that as a writer he creates anything.

It is problematic, too, to describe the essayist, as Scott Russell Sanders wonderfully does, as "the singular first person," extolling his individuality and even uniqueness in a world gone bland, monochromatic, and indiscriminate. Modesty resides just this side of self-assertiveness, a lesson Sanders might have learned from his mentor Thoreau, who, while proclaiming the modest life and crying in all things for "simplicity, simplicity, simplicity," loses his balance, makes rash assertions, and exacts quite immodest demands of us all. More successful, ultimately, and more effective are the writers who turn modesty into self-effacement. E. B. White practically made a career of doing so, and Sam Pickering has recently followed suit, constantly poking fun at himself, reveling, in fact, in his own unsuitableness and ineptitude. Particularly impressive is the modesty shown by Richard Selzer, for instance in "An Absence of Windows," a deflation of the surgeon's ego that lays bare the writer's own vulnerability and complicities. The magnificent final sentences express the humility Selzer incarnates even with the surgeon's awesome powers: "a man is entitled to the temple of his preference. Mine lies out on a prairie, wondering up at Heaven. Or in a many windowed operating room where, just outside the panes of glass, cows graze, and the stars shine down upon my carpentry."[10] Montaigne, I imagine, smiles and shines down upon this worthy practitioner.

I hear the same strain when Virginia Woolf introduces her 1925 collection of essays *The Common Reader*. Her opening sentence invokes Dr. Johnson and the important recognition that "might well be written up in all those rooms, too humble to be called libraries, yet full of books, where the pursuit of reading is carried on by private people." She then quotes Johnson, from his *Life of Gray*: "'I rejoice to concur with the common reader; for by the common sense of readers, uncorrupted by literary prejudices, after all the refinements of subtilty and the dogmatism of learning, must be finally decided all claim to poetical honours.'"[11] Here, modesty conjoins with the experiential and the empirical, as well as with the common and that littleness of which Phillip Lopate speaks. What Woolf herself proceeds to write, in this brief introduction, connects "the common reader" with that humility Eliot extolled in Charles Whibley:

> The common reader, as Dr. Johnson implies, differs from the critic and the scholar. He is worse educated, and nature has not gifted him so generously. He reads for his own pleasure rather than to

impart knowledge or correct the opinions of others. Above all, he is guided by an instinct to create for himself, out of whatever odds and ends he can come by, some kind of whole—a portrait of a man, a sketch of an age, a theory of the art of writing. He never ceases, as he reads, to run up some rickety and ramshackle fabric which shall give him the temporary satisfaction of looking sufficiently like the real object to allow of affection, laughter, and argument. Hasty, inaccurate, and superficial, snatching now this poem, now that scrap of old furniture without caring where he finds it or of what nature it may be so long as it serves his purpose and rounds his structure, his deficiencies as a critic are too obvious to be pointed out. . . .[12]

The battle now becomes joined, for as Clara Claiborne Park has recently written in *Rejoining the Common Reader: Essays, 1962–1990*, the common does not at all equate with the trivial, the superficial, or the insignificant. On the contrary, for Park, the common reader is she or he who, like readers in Johnson's day and unlike today's academicized and professionalized readers, "expect 'just representations of general nature' that will help them understand their own lives and the world more truly." More specifically, Park defines the common reader as one who has "not gone stale on the eternal questions." It is he who asks the large questions of meaning and significance, turning to literature in a personal, engaged manner for understanding of self and world.[13]

Cynthia Ozick puts the matter in another way in "The Riddle of the Ordinary." This is a close, sophisticated analysis of the meaning of "the ordinary," with which the essay is intimately related, although it is none of her concern to say so. It also serves as a vigorous defense of her Judaism. In the essay, Ozick cautions that we be wary of easily embracing the ordinary, tempting as it is. Ozick's ultimate point is differential, addressing significant and conflicting ways of interpreting creation; she locates just here, in fact, "the deepest danger our human brains are subject to." She writes, "If we are enjoined to live in the condition of noticing all things—or, to put it more extremely but more exactly, in the condition of awe—*how can we keep ourselves from sliding off from awe at God's Creation to worship of God's Creation?*"[14] On this point, she says with some pride, the Jew is "famously stiff-necked," holding to a position "uncompromisingly pure and impatient with self-deception." For him, and her, Christianity is a sad mistake:

> . . . nothing but the Creator, no substitute and no mediator. The Creator is not contained in his own Creation; the Creator is incarnate in nothing, and is free of any image or imagining. God is not any part of Nature, or in any part of Nature; God is not any man, or in any man. When we praise Nature or man or any experience or work of man, we are worshiping the Creator, and the Creator alone. Those of us who sing the praises of the ordinary are, however, on the way to idolatry.[15]

A strong admirer of Ozick's writing—"The Seam of the Snail" is exquisite, its sentences as "comely" as "muscular," and "A Drugstore in Winter" shows, at many levels, just how creative the essay can be—I recognize that her argument demands her conclusion; but I find it, so stated, immodest, lacking humility. Still, Ozick shows us the question, and we are indebted to her for pointing to the ultimate implications of our choices. To adopt the essay's mode, to train our attention on the ordinary, is fraught with serious implications that have very rarely been recognized, let alone explored. The stakes are high here, in this matter of that slight thing, the second-class citizen that we term the essay.

The ordinary, the common, the humble, the modest—they variously describe aspects of the essay, the essayistic character, and the form's space, if you will. But there always, or nearly always, appears a tension, such that alongside the modest, for instance, some pretension or vanity rears its ugly head. Even Selzer's magnificent last sentence in "An Absence of Windows" reveals some tension, for the final word "carpentry" points in potentially contrary directions: toward the possibility that surgery is no more than glorified woodworking, and at the same time toward the quite different and far grander resonance with the work of Christ, the humble carpenter. Now I am not here proposing a deconstruction, whereby a textual "description" subverts an authorial "declaration"; my interest is simpler, focusing on tension and intent on exploring the implications it bears.

In the second epigraph to this chapter, the Hungarian materialist philosopher Georg Lukács treats the condition of the essay. His own essay, titled "On the Nature and Form of the Essay," appeared in 1910, rather modestly addressed as "a letter to a friend." Lukács's considerable contribution consists in probing the situation Ozick would later analyze in a more general context: he argues that, in the essay, there is always a tension—although he does not use the term—between its lowly claims and ordinary interests and its larger and great ambitions. (The relationship between the ordinary and the extraordinary, which Ozick forcefully describes, does not concern him.) The term that Lukács uses for this situation is *irony*, and it has been picked up and embraced by later commentators, particularly of the Continental stripe (e.g., Geoffrey H. Hartman). "That irony which we find in the writings of every truly great essayist," writes Lukács, "consists in the critic always speaking about the ultimate problems of life, but in a tone which implies that he is only discussing pictures and books, only the inessential and pretty ornaments of real life—and even then not their innermost substance but only their beautiful and useless surface."[16]

Lukács focuses on the critical essay, although at times his interest appears to extend to all essays. In any case, he begins from the essay's "second-class citizenship," a term made famous by (the ironic) E. B. White: "most people have to believe that the writings of the essayists are produced only in order to explain books and pictures, to facilitate their understanding."[17] The essay is, in other words, secondary in status and being. But wait, says Lukács: the essay only appears to be modest, or feigns its secondariness. The essayist's tone exists in tension with its ultimate aims because the essayist is aiming at greater game. The essay, in any case, remains grounded, each incarnation of the form "appear[ing] to be removed as far as possible from life." Meanwhile, in the midst of tension between modesty and arrogance, traceable to Montaigne's adaptation of the word "essays" for his *Abbau*-ist writings, the essayist "ironically adapts himself to this smallness—the eternal smallness of the most profound work of the intellect in face of life—and even emphasize[s] it with ironic modesty."[18] Who would not be tempted by Lukács's seductive argument? It is snakelike in its attractiveness, based in pride and appealing to pride, as well as to residual questions of perceived justice and fairness. We all like to believe our work is important and anticipate some recognition of its value, even if it is mean (often especially when it is so). I detect no desperation in Lukács, but I do think the scales become tipped; he loses the balance that is so hard to maintain, his assaying of the essay's assaying just missing the mark.

The essayist is nothing if not self-critical, alert to the deceptions that mark the self's squeamish existence. He thus turns his skeptical eye inward and probes his motives and desires alike, knowing that the mote in another's eye can easily obscure the beam in his own. White's wonderful "Death of a Pig" movingly represents the essayist's complicities and duplicities, exposing himself entirely. Under few illusions (finally), the essayist seems to me to cast his eye downward, watching where he is going, rather than upward to imagine ethereal things; he is about as far from the inhabitants of Swift's Laputa as you would want, as rarely tempted to theorize as to pontificate. Among the essayists I have read and re-read, I sense neither the aspiration Lukács posits nor the ambition he describes. It is admittedly a matter of some delicacy.

I will insist that indirectness attends the essay, but in Lukács I find next to none. Consider Belloc's aforementioned "The Mowing of a Field." From its simple, descriptive beginning and its quite mundane subject, Belloc moves outward to a general social and cultural critique, his prey large. But he moves steadily, without irony; there is no pretension toward "the ultimate." Instead of irony, something else pertains, something subtler. It is apparent in the tone and manner.

Belloc modulates from topic to topic, from the description of the valley in the south of England to which he returns after a long absence, to that of the art of mowing, beginning with the sharpening of the blade. It all fits, including the end account of the way to buy land or a pig, and what holds this remarkable, unassuming essay together is respect, its major theme. Belloc not only discusses respect (although the word itself never once is used), but he also shows it in action (sometimes indirectly through negative example) and represents it incarnate in himself. The following passage centers Belloc's thematic interests; it is the essay's climactic moment, rhetorically powerful, highly charged, and nearly heroic in its savage indignation:

> Mowing well and mowing badly—or rather not mowing at all—are separated by very little; as is also true of writing verse, of playing the fiddle, and of dozens of other things, but of nothing more than of believing. For the bad or young or untaught mower without tradition, the mower Promethean, the mower original and contemptuous of the past, does all these things: He leaves great crescents of grass uncut. He digs the point of the scythe hard into the ground with a jerk. He loosens the handles and even the fastening of the blade. He twists the blade with his blindness, he blunts the blade, he chips it, dulls it, or breaks it clean off at the tip. If anyone is standing by he cuts him in the ankle.

The grammatical tumble, with its violence and violation, reflects Belloc's barely controlled contempt, and given the strength of his feeling the rhythm is appropriate, deserved. He follows with another riotous sentence and follows that with one whose subordinate clause quickly turns quiet: "He sweeps up into the air wildly, with nothing to resist his stroke. He drags up earth with the grass, which is like making the meadow bleed." The reserve of these last words finds its mark, chilling the reader. Belloc then turns positive: "But the good mower who does things just as they should be done and have been for a hundred thousand years, falls into none of these fooleries. He goes forward very steadily, his scythe-blade just barely missing the ground, every grass falling; the swish and rhythm of his mowing are always the same."[19]

Such thematically resonant and rhetorically magnificent passages sneak up on you in Belloc's essay; you expect neither such elegance nor such grandeur of thought. And in fact, the manner here—this sneakiness—better describes the essay's procedure generally than does irony. The importance lies on the surface, not below it but lateral to the mundane occasion and to accounts of the quite ordinary. That importance derives ultimately from the mind, Belloc's, that sees, understands, and grasps, probing and pursuing implications, all in a manner unassuming, restrained, and poised until it can no longer bear the moral offensiveness against which it then appropriately proclaims. Nothing appears to be left unsaid or merely implied—it's all out in the open, not apparent only in spirit. The literal rules here, manifest in a statement such as that concerning praying, which bothers those like Lukács inclined to the purely transcendent: "mowing should be like one's prayers—all of a sort and always the same, and so made that you can establish a monotony and work them, as it were, with half your mind: that happier half, the half that does not bother."[20] Missing here, sadly for Romantics, is interiorization.

We are conditioned now to seek beneath the surface and above the literal; we are transcendentalists and spiritualists never more than in our extreme materialism. Irony thus appeals as a way to describe the essay's manner. It actually works, though, in a contrary manner, surface-level terms revealing the importance that lies right there, in front of your eyes.

I call this "sneaky" because it surprises—who would expect so much from writing about the mowing of a field, a piece of chalk

(Chesterton), chasing one's hat (Beerbohm), or the death of a pig or of a moth? There is stealth involved in the essayistic endeavor, a certain furtiveness, even trickiness. Nothing matches the sneakiness of hiding nothing.

The elusive quality I am laboring to describe is not to be confused with the notion of "hiding in plain sight." There is neither evasion nor pretense in the essay. Rather, its importance emerges as the essayist writes and as the reader reads, appearing as a dimension not above it but of and within it—immanent, in other words. While sneaky in my terms, the essay lacks the subtlety and perhaps the sophistication that Lukács attributes to it. Some essays, to be sure, may approach that level and kind of ambition—say, those of Lukács himself and of Theodor Adorno and Walter Benjamin—but in so doing the essay becomes very nearly unrecognizable. So concerned with meaning, rather than represented experience, it veers toward philosophy. The tone and manner of the essay is different: lighter, rooted, familiar—without rendering the essay less important or significant.

THE ESSAY will remain second-class—as long as it is true to itself, true to the venerable tradition that began more than four hundred years ago with Montaigne. You can thus say that its status "down the line" from the novel, the poem, and the play is the essay's own fault, for it presumes to be nothing else. The essayist "not only must be content" in his role of "second-class citizen," as E. B. White averred, but is. While his ambition is not so grand as Lukács postulated, the form he or she practices has a profound significance, not least by means and because of its wisdom, modesty, and humility.

HOME-COSMOGRAPHY
THE RENAISSANCE BASIS OF THE ESSAY

∽

> "Direct your eye inwards, and you'll find
> A thousand regions in your mind
> Yet undiscovered. Travel them, and be
> Expert in home-cosmography."

... *If you would learn to speak all tongues and conform to the customs of all nations, if you would travel farther than all travelers, be naturalized in all climes, and cause the Sphinx to dash her head against a stone, even obey the precept of the old philosopher, and Explore thyself. Herein are demanded the eye and the nerve. Only the defeated and deserters go to the wars, cowards that run away and enlist. Start now on the farthest western way, which does not pause at the Mississippi or the Pacific, nor conduct toward a worn-out China or Japan, but leads on direct a tangent to this sphere, summer and winter, day and night, sun down, moon down, and at last earth down too.*

Henry David Thoreau, *Walden*, quoting William Habington, "To My Honoured Friend Sir Ed. P. Knight," in *Castara* (1634)

∽

FEW WOULD DISPUTE that the essay as we know it began with Michel de Montaigne's first edition of his *Essais* in 1580. Significant predecessors had appeared in ancient Rome, the prose writings of Seneca and Plutarch in particular, and in the Orient there had been the tenth-century meditations of Sei Shonagon known as *The Pillow Book* and the fourteenth-century *Essays in Idleness* by Kenko. But in truth, these last, so-called essays that are part of a tradition known as "following the brush," bear little resemblance to Montaigne's work, which was soon followed in England by Francis Bacon's ten brief *Essays* in 1597 (later greatly expanded, just as Montaigne expanded his), Sir William Cornwallis's *Essays* in 1600, and John Donne's *Devotions* in 1624. Whatever the similarity between the prose of Seneca and Plutarch and that of Europeans a millennium and a half later, there was no direct link and certainly no ongoing tradition. Most important, nothing like the self-explorations of Montaigne had ever appeared. His "efforts," mere trials or attempts, were genuinely different, representing something new.

For this reason, Montaigne understood the necessity of both explaining and defending his manner and subject in his apologia "Of Practice." In this essay he writes confidently and not at all defensively, beginning with an account of a fall from his horse that very nearly cost him his life. He follows with reflections on sleep, its relation to death, and its propaedeutic and propagating value, and he turns to the matter of his writing about it all:

This account of so trivial an event would be rather pointless, were it not for the instruction that I have derived from it for myself; for in truth, in order to get used to the idea of death, I find there is nothing like coming close to it. Now as Pliny says, each man is a good education to himself, provided he has the capacity to spy on himself from close up. What I write here is not my teaching, but my study; it is not a lesson for others, but for me.

More is to be said, however, and needs to be. So Montaigne opens his defense with a frank acknowledgment of the new and controversial nature of his undertaking, this studying of himself on paper, scrupulously and microscopically—the tension is unmistakable. Montaigne's description of exactly what his innovation consists of is as good a description of the essay as has ever been managed (I quote it again, therefore):

> It is a thorny undertaking, and more so than it seems, to follow a movement so wandering as that of our mind, to penetrate the opaque depths of its innermost folds, to pick out and immobilize the innumerable flutterings that agitate it. And it is a new and extraordinary amusement, which withdraws us from the ordinary occupations of the world, yes, even from those most recommended.[1]

The object of his writing, Montaigne insists, is self-discovery, or, rather, self-exploration. Cornwallis, a few years later, made his essaying an "apprenticeship in self-knowledge."[2] As he develops the point, Montaigne reverts to defending writing and publishing his results:

> It is many years now that I have had only myself as object of my thoughts, that I have been examining and studying only myself; and if I study anything else, it is in order promptly to apply it to myself,

or rather within myself. And it does not seem to me that I am making a mistake if—as is done in the other sciences, which are incomparably less useful—I impart what I have learned in this one, though I am hardly satisfied with the progress I have made in it. There is no description equal in difficulty, or certainly in usefulness, to the description of oneself. Even so one must spruce up, even so one must present oneself in an orderly arrangement, if one would go out in public. Now, I am constantly adorning myself, for I am constantly describing myself.[3]

With the last two sentences here, as I have said, Montaigne also reveals the little-acknowledged tension so prominent in the essay as to be characteristic of the form, tension that is ultimately traceable to the form's way of uniting immanence and transcendence and of deriving meaning from, in, and through experience.

Continuing, Montaigne specifies even more clearly how his writing is new: "I expose myself entire: my portrait is a cadaver on which the veins, the muscles, and the tendons appear at a glance, each part in its place.... It is not my deeds that I write down; it is myself, it is my essence."[4] As he writes—and as I hope my generous quoting has shown—Montaigne is taking "a line out for a walk." You sense him reflecting, turning ideas over in his mind, pursuing a thought here, caressing it there, assaying as he tries it on—thinking *in the process of* writing. The progress is not linear—and it shouldn't be, for the essayist represents his attempts to "get it down right."

IN MONTAIGNE'S EFFORTS, in Bacon's and in Cornwallis's, the essayist appears to be a product of the Renaissance. He maps the microcosm just as cartographers were beginning to chart the macrocosm, the latter efforts made possible by the voyages of the great explorers Columbus, Magellan, Cortez, de Gama, and others. The exploration that Montaigne initiated of self—or "home"—was made possible by new thinking and new freedoms that were challenging and toppling hitherto-accepted ways of doing things. Authority was in question everywhere, and in so many senses a new world was being born. A certain skepticism arose that befitted the individualism that was banging on the door of institution after institution. Recovery of the great learning of the ancient world abetted the effort, the resulting Humanism focusing attention on grammar, rhetoric, poetry, history, and moral philosophy. Attention thus shifted, as that later Humanist and essayist Alexander Pope put it, from the ways of God to those of man, the latter becoming man's "proper study." Thus Humanism wrought a preoccupation with the art of writing and the art of living: "Knowledge that was only indirectly or not at all relevant to linguistic or to life-style was only indirectly or not at all relevant to the Humanist's concerns."[5] As Montaigne engaged in an *Abbau*, or deconstruction, of a tired rhetorical tradition,[6] he offered what has been termed "personal philosophy," successfully challenging one tradition after another, a wily individual becoming a virtual one-man wrecking crew.

Indeed, "the main force of his writing would ultimately not come from 'elsewhere,' but from his own freshly and directly experienced thoughts and passions, with a minimum of borrowed, alien artifice."[7] The façon of living the Humanists were concerned with had been made clear by Erasmus, who died in 1536, three years after Montaigne was born. Interested little in a man's occupation or his social representation, Erasmus taught the student of human beings and of the art of living to look beyond appearance and to look long at "their naked selves," as he put it in his *Praise of Folly*. You must, that is,

> lay a man open, look *through* what he is to the public, and see how he lives in the intimacy of his own soul and his own household. In doing this you see the reality of the man, not simply "the part he is to act ... on the stage." When you are laying a man bare you are not asking whether he is a king or soldier or even what his scientific and religious convictions are in detail; you are asking, "What woman would be content with such a husband? Who would invite such a guest? ... " The test of his real worth involves his way of feeling, thinking, and acting in his constant, intimate relationships with himself, his family, and his friends.[8]

Of course, the man Montaigne lays bare is himself, his great contribution to the moral enterprise that runs from Erasmus through his great admirer Pope. Montaigne himself makes the point regarding this *"façon simple, naturelle et ordinaire"* in writing in the essay "Of the Art of Discussion": "every day I amuse myself reading authors without any care for their learning, looking for their style, not their subject. Just as I seek the company of some famous mind, not to have him teach me, but to come to know him."[9]

Montaigne withdrew from the public world, where he had been a figure of some prominence: Mayor of Bordeaux, counselor to Henry of Navarre as well as to the king. The public strife of his difficult time barely makes its way into his *essais*. The richness we find there is not of culture or history but of this now-private individual: "the richness of a person who had withdrawn in his heart from a sick public situation so that he could *be* more fully, more vigorously, than that situation could permit."[10] In this, his writing and his living are the mirror-image of each other: "Our great and glorious masterpiece," he wrote, "is to live appropriately," the language of one façon transferable to the other. Moreover, the writing becomes, in this first essayist, "both a path *of* knowing and a path *to* knowing"; as I write, wrote Montaigne, I am "forming my life," which is "the greatest task of all."[11] In him, the essay became "a medium for the art of the living," a point echoed by perhaps his greatest American successor, Ralph Waldo Emerson: "Then I dare; I also will essay to be."[12]

This entirely new emphasis on being cannot be overstated. Before Montaigne, in Homer and Dante for instance, the represented goal is understanding. Montaigne shifts that focus from the capacity of the mind attuned to a tradition to that of the individual in all his life, even shorn of tradition, which, anyhow, appears to be sick. For Montaigne, self-understanding does not mean, as it does later for Pope ("Know then thyself; presume not God to scan; / The proper study of mankind is man"), awareness of one's limitations and finite capacities, and especially his proneness to error. Montaigne's aim is not self-correction but "home-cosmography." The impact is ethical, to be sure, but ethical in a strictly limited sort of way. Being emerges from and by means of this self-discovery and mapping, rather than via comprehension of the order outside the individual and, indeed, outside man.

Experience is the great Renaissance teacher, not the Church. Reading enlightens and educates; it is, of course, of immense value; and Montaigne is not only always reading but also remembering. The standard, however, by which he weighs claims to truth is his experience. The essay was, historically, the first form to take the experience of the individual and make it the stuff of literature; the novel soon followed suit.

The Reformation is, of course, a crucial episode of the Renaissance. In fact, the emergence of the authority of the private individual is particularly clear in the successful reform effort to effect the "priesthood of all believers." What the Reformation wrought reveals much about the Renaissance and the epochal shifts that soon followed.

I know of no clearer or sharper account of the issues that were at stake in the Reformation as it relates to the essay than John Dryden's *Religio Laici or A Laymans Faith*, in which you can feel the lingering effects of the English civil war and of the Puritan experiment, offspring of the Reformation. Dryden paints an unflattering picture of the Catholic absolutism and corruption that led to Luther's reform efforts. For Dryden, reading—one's relation to the printed word—becomes a metaphor for one's way of religious, political, and cultural existence:

> In times o'ergrown with Rust and Ignorance,
> A gainfull Trade their Clergy did advance:
> When want of Learning kept the *Laymen* low,
> And none but *Priests* were *Authoriz'd* to *know*:
> When what small Knowledge was, in them did dwell;
> And he a *God* who cou'd but *Reade* or *Spell*;
> Then *Mother Church* did mightily prevail:
> She parcel'd out the Bible by *retail*:
> But still *expounded* what She *sold* or *gave*;
> To keep it in *her Power* to *Damn* and *Save*:
> *Scripture* was *scarce*, and as the Market went,
> Poor *Laymen* took *Salvation* on *Content*;
> As needy men take Money, good or bad:

> *God's* Word they had not, but the *Priests* they had.
> Yet, whate'er *false Conveyances* they made,
> The *Lawyer* still was *certain* to be paid.
> In those dark times they learn'd their knack so well,
> That by long use they grew *Infallible*:
> At last, a knowing Age began t' enquire
> If *they* the *Book*, or *That* did *them* inspire:
> And, making narrower search they found, thô late,
> That what they thought the *Priest's*, was *Their* Estate:
> Taught by the *Will produc'd*, (the written Word)
> How long they had been *cheated* on *Record*.
> Then, every man who saw the Title fair,
> Claim'd a Child's part, and put in for a Share:
> Consulted Soberly his private good;
> And sav'd himself as cheap as e'er he cou'd. (370–97)[13]

Before the Reformation, the situation of the laity was intolerable: they had no direct access to or experience of Scripture, having to rely on a priesthood represented here as self-serving and corrupt. Dryden thus presents the Reformation as a necessity, although one whose consequences soon became catastrophic. The response of laymen to their new freedom was how the oppressed always respond when they are wrenched into power and authority (although to say so is not at all to justify their oppression and the brutality with which it is meted out):

> 'Tis true, my Friend, (and far be Flattery hence)
> This good had full as bad a Consequence:
> The *Book* thus put in every vulgar hand,

THE RENAISSANCE BASIS OF THE ESSAY

> Which each presum'd he best cou'd understand,
> The *Common Rule* was made the *common Prey*;
> And at the mercy of the *Rabble* lay. (398–403)

Dryden then specifies how "the *private Spirit*" functioned when liberated and made the arbiter of textual and interpretive decisions:

> The tender Page with horney Fists was gaul'd;
> And he was gifted most that loudest baul'd:
> The *Spirit* gave the *Doctoral Degree*:
> And every member of a *Company*
> Was of *his Trade*, and of the *Bible free*.
> Plain *Truths* enough for needfull *use* they found;
> But men wou'd still be itching to *expound*:
> Each was ambitious of th' obscurest place,
> No measure ta'n from *Knowledge*, all from GRACE.
> *Study* and *Pains* were now no more their Care;
> *Texts* were explain'd by *Fasting*, and by *Prayer*:
> This was the Fruit the *private Spirit* brought;
> Occasion'd by *great Zeal*, and *little Thought*.
> While Crouds unlearn'd, with rude Devotion warm,
> About the Sacred Viands buz and swarm,
> The *Fly-blown Text* creates a *crawling Brood*;
> And turns to *Maggots* what was meant for *Food*.
> A Thousand daily Sects rise up, and dye;
> A Thousand more the perish'd Race supply. (404–22)

Dryden's imagery shows the depth of his contempt. Although he describes a "layman's faith" congruent with his longtime anticlericalism, he treats the sectarians much more rudely and savagely than he does the priests. At any rate, he concludes on the note with which the verse paragraph began, a version of the familiar lament that "new presbyter is but old priest writ large," and the result is the same whether the layman is shackled by the clergy or allows his own will to traduce "the *Will produc'd*":

> So all we make of Heavens discover'd Will
> Is, not to have it, or to use it ill.
> The Danger's much the same; on several Shelves
> If *others* wreck *us*, or *we* wreck our *selves*. (423–26)

The battle of wills knows no end or limits, and Dryden, spokesman for the King and the Established Church, recognizes and distrusts the human willfulness that was manifest in the usurpation of authority by the private individual.

THE CHOICE here of *Religio Laici* as a source no doubt seems odd; a poem written well after the Renaissance, it speaks partially, hardly objectively, and takes a side inimical to the direction Western culture was taking. That it offers a position counter to the movement that produced the essay is, however, just the point. And in truth, *Religio Laici* is important to us for a number of reasons, with implications and insights we can ill afford to ignore.

To begin: Despite the centrality to the poem of reading and textual interpretation, no one (to my knowledge) has noticed that "layman" may be read as a metaphor, for instance of "the common reader." That is, in fact, "layman" can be read not only as the person to whom *Religio Laici* is addressed but also as the position of the poet: he thus distinguishes between the cleric or professional and persons like himself:

> The few, by Nature form'd, with Learning fraught,
> Born to instruct, as others to be taught,
> Must Study well the Sacred Page; and see
> Which Doctrine, this, or that, does best agree
> With the whole Tenour of the Work Divine:
> And plainlyest points to Heaven's reveal'd Design:
> *Which* Exposition flows from *genuine Sense*;
> And which is *forc'd* by *Wit* and *Eloquence*. (326–33)

The layman's task is different, easier; his interests are neither professional nor scholarly but personal. For his purpose—ultimately, knowledge of the path to salvation—the text is sufficiently clear and is in need of no interpreter or intermediary (I have a hard time restricting Dryden's meaning to just one book):

> The *Book*'s a *Common Largess* to *Mankind*;
> Not more for *them*, than *every* Man design'd;
> The *welcome News* is in the *Letter* found;
> The *Carrier*'s not Commission'd to *expound*.
> It *speaks* it *Self*, and what it does contain,
> In all things *needfull* to be *known*, is *plain*. (364–69)

Dryden's lay position here anticipates Virginia Woolf's description and embrace of "the common reader," which I quoted in the previous chapter; it also recalls Woolf's passionate defense of the ordinary reader in "How Should One Read a Book?" There is a difference, though, and a significant one: whereas Dryden proceeds from an assumption regarding the self-sufficiency of the text, Woolf takes a more radically Protestant position, refusing even to consult any outside authority. Dryden would condemn her opening salvo: "The only advice, indeed, that one person can give another about reading is to take no advice, to follow your own instincts, to use your own reason, to come to your own conclusions."[14] Dryden tempers freedom with the recommendation—or requirement—that the layman "learn what unsuspected Ancients say" (436) when passages are doubtful and meaning is in question and then, "after hearing what our Church can say,/ If still our Reason runs another way,/ That private Reason 'tis more Just to curb" (445–46). Woolf would admit no such turn nor brook any such mediator; the following passage comes immediately after the quotation just above:

> If this is agreed between us, then I feel at liberty to put forward a few ideas and suggestions because you will not allow them to fetter that independence which is the most important quality that a reader can possess. After all, what laws can be laid down about books? The battle of Waterloo was certainly fought on a certain day; but is *Hamlet* a better play than *Lear*? Nobody can say. Each must decide that question for himself. To admit authorities, however heavily furred and gowned, into our libraries and let them tell us how to read, what to read, what value to place upon what we read, is to destroy the spirit of freedom which is the breath of those sanctuaries. Everywhere else we may be bound by laws and conventions—there we have none.[15]

The relation of this passage to *Religio Laici* is, I trust, sufficiently clear. Woolf's belief in the reader's absolute freedom from outside authority is an instance of the democracy Dryden feared, one that within five years of publishing his work drove him to the Church of Rome.

Implicit in Woolf's essay is the connection between "the common reader" and the amateur, another analogue of the layman. The last sentences very nearly render that connection explicit: Woolf says, concluding, that she has often dreamt that on the Day of Judgment "the Almighty will turn to Peter and will say, not without a certain envy when He sees us coming with our books under our arms, 'Look, these need no reward. We have nothing to give them here. They have *loved* reading'" (italics mine).[16] The amateur is, thus, also Dryden's layman who is, as Woolf said introducing *The Common Reader*, "worse educated" than the critic and the scholar, and not so generously "gifted." Although he may be "hasty, inaccurate, and superficial," this common reader-amateur-layman "reads for his own pleasure"—and, I would add, for his own benefit, driven not by professional ambitions and narrow, specialized, technical interests, but by familiar, moral, and often religious ones. He looks for the big picture and asks the difficult questions of meaning and personal significance.

One further connection remains to be made, and that is between the composite common reader-amateur-layman and the essayist, a relation already implicit in the foregoing paragraphs. Independence of spirit and thinking lies at the heart of all four, along with a commitment to individual authority, however measured. The point has been well made by novelist-philosopher-essayist William H. Gass; before dismissing the (definite) article as an "awful object" and the essay's "opposite," Gass makes explicit the essayist's amateur status and nature, and implicit his lay character:

> A certain scientific or philosophical rigor is . . . foreign to the essay. . . . Consequently, jargon in an essay is like a worm in fruit; one wants to bite around the offending hunk or spit it out. The apparatus of the scholar is generally kept hid; frequently quotations are not even identified (we *both* know who said *that*, and anyway its origin doesn't matter). The essayist is an amateur, a Virginia Woolf who has merely done a little reading up; he is not out for profit (even when paid), or promotion (even if it occurs); but is interested solely in the essay's special *art*. Meditation is the essence of it; it measures meanings; makes maps; exfoliates. The essay is unhurried (although Bacon's aren't); it browses among books; it enjoys an idea like a fine wine; it thumbs through things. It turns round and round upon its topic, exposing this aspect and then that; proposing possibilities, reciting opinions, disposing of prejudice and even of the simple truth itself—as too undeveloped, not yet of an interesting age.[17]

It's hard to do better than Gass, doubtful that you'll find a surer, truer sense of the essay's complex nature.

Although I don't believe it has been remarked, the essayist is not just an amateur but also, as Gass suggests, also a layman and, as Virginia Woolf herself suggests, a common reader. The essayist's field is broad and open, not narrow and devoted to only one type of crop. And at this point some additional distinctions must be made. To begin with, we acknowledge the fact and difference of Bacon's essays—and so of important and crucial deviations from the Frenchman Montaigne. Bacon is distinctly English, as is Dryden and as is the essay that we customarily think of as experimental and "of" or "on" something. I am tempted to call the difference between Montaigne and Bacon that between the personal and the familiar.

To be sure, Montaigne pens essays called "Of Solitude" and "Of Books," and yet, as Graham Good writes, using Walter Pater's line from the "conclusion" of *The Renaissance,* for Montaigne, "Not the fruit of experience, but experience itself, is the end."[18] Bacon, on the other hand, offers his version of the essay as "fruits" rather than "experiences," or, in Good's words, as "the results of inquiry, not the process of inquiry." Thus Bacon's essays appear more carefully crafted, more structurally integral, more shaped and formed, whereas Montaigne's appear rambling, "loose, exploratory, and digressive."[19] Accordingly, we are, many of us, tempted to assign to Montaigne the essence of the essay and relegate Bacon not as derivative but as veering from the Frenchman's meandering way into something formal. The old distinction between product and process emerges, as indicated in Graham Good's distinction. I think that this difference brings us to the heart of the matter of the essay *as artistic structure.* I am inclined to say, with perhaps all other commentators of whatever stripe, that the essay is a wandering and wondering form, but as soon as I say so, I know that I must pull back and qualify.

Teaching the writing of essays humbles me and makes me cautious, for a fledgling essayist who presents a ramble almost always offers nothing more than self-expression, not reaching craft, let alone art. So I find myself advising a free-wheeling first draft, essentially the process of finding one's way, which *must* be followed by at least a second draft, a complete revision of the first, one that proceeds from the discovery made. Process thus turns into product.

After all, even an essay that most resembles a ramble, for instance William Hazlitt's well-known "On Going a Journey," belies its apparently loose and carefree nature: the first paragraph does, indeed, extend to three pages, and the last is full of dashes, suggesting fresh starts and sudden, even unplanned stops, but the deeply analytical and philosophical third paragraph, summarizing the argument for the mind's characteristically associative operations, makes clear the author's quite conscious and firm control of the essay's movement.

Venture very far in the direction of process, and you get the lyric; do so toward product, and you have the article that Gass excoriates, formal to the point of stuffiness and exclusion. Perhaps the reason we cannot define the essay is that it lies "between," pulled in contrary directions, toward process and product, experience and meaning, self and other. It does indeed seem to "hang somewhere on a line between two sturdy poles," as Edward Hoagland has written, but I would describe the poles differently.[20] Rather than "this is what I think, and this is what I am," they are various analogues of the differences and oppositions we have been discussing—and tension is fundamental.

Then, to call Montaigne "the father of the essay" is to tell a partial story, no more nor less complete than honoring Francis Bacon with the title. The essay, rather, hangs on a line between these two quite sturdy poles. But we are not done yet—not even with the suggestiveness of *Religio Laici*. For Bacon, like Dryden, advises the "middle temper," akin to that *via media* the poet embraces between the authoritarianism of the Church of Rome and the personal indulgence of the dissenting sects: "This strategy of avoiding extremes is characteristic of Bacon, and provides a typically neat rhetorical pattern as well, a trial consisting of opposite errors with the truth in the middle."[21] Such a procedure is, of course, also characteristically English, reflecting, among other things, the nature of the Established Church and the wonderfully British way of avoiding extremes. I wrote long ago of the essay's "both/and" nature, and I would still, although at that time I was thinking, rather, of Derrida and deconstruction, but now of its essential *tension*. If the essay appears a both/and creation, it is just as clearly, if not more so, a neither/nor.

We may, then, locate the essay as that crossing between self and other, experience and meaning, process and product, form and formlessness that I mentioned earlier and that I shall elaborate in due course. It is not so much protean or shape-shifting as pushed and pulled, caught between contending forces—and seeking composure. The ideal essay would exist at dead-center of this line, but I suspect there is no such and never will be, for this famous "greased pig" does not and cannot be still; indeed, it animadverts against the very notion of "ideal"—as in its individualism it struggles against individualism. The way to palatable individualism lies, the essay suggests, in, through, and by means of its (Renaissance) tradition.

THE MOST SELF-CENTERED OF FORMS?
DISTINGUISHING THE ESSAY

The essayist is a self-liberated man, sustained by the childish belief that everything he thinks about, everything that happens to him, is of general interest. . . . Only a person who is congenitally self-centered has the effrontery and the stamina to write essays. . . .

I think some people find the essay the last resort of the egoist, a much too self-conscious and self-serving form for their taste; they feel that it is presumptuous of a writer to assume that his little excursions or his small observations will interest the reader. There is some justice in their complaint. I have always been aware that I am by nature self-absorbed and egoistical; to write of myself to the extent I have done indicates a too great attention to my own life, not enough to the lives of others.

E. B. White, foreword, *Essays*

"THE STENCH OF EGO" attends the essayist. Montaigne is clear that in his new-fangled *Essais* he "had only myself as object of my thoughts," "constantly describing myself," portraying "chiefly" his "cogitations," and thereby writing down himself, his "essence."¹ Following suit, Thoreau announced on the opening page of *Walden* that he would be talking mainly about himself: "In most books, the *I*, or first person, is omitted; in this it will be retained; that, in respect to egotism, is the main difference. We commonly do not remember that it is, after all, always the first person that is speaking."² In a meandering line from Thoreau, whom he honored on the hundredth anniversary of *Walden*'s publication with the magnificent essay "A Slight Sound at Evening," E. B. White offered the oft-quoted summary account of the essayist's egoism and of the form's self-centeredness. In paying homage to the essay's "onlie begetter" as White nods toward and graciously acknowledges tradition, he perhaps inadvertently links Montaigne with egotism—a brand that the "father of the essay" can hardly escape.

Although Montaigne is obviously implicated, Thoreau can only problematically be accused, for if I read his statement opening *Walden* correctly, he denies that his use of the first person signals egotism—after all, whether the "I" is present or absent, "it is always the first person that is speaking." Moreover, as Lawrence Buell has made abundantly clear, *Walden* gradually and deliberately moves outward and away from self as Thoreau becomes more and more focused on the world of Walden Pond.³ And as to White, I can hear only irony in his delicate, self-effacing foreword to the *Essays*: there is such lightness of touch there that White appears to grant the essay's and the essayist's concern with self in a manner just playful enough to make his (self) criticism fall short of rigid and absolute. Of course, in calling attention to and granting self-consciousness and self-interestedness, this passage bares another dimension of the self's preoccupation. Rather, though, than outright or heavy-handed, the account is sneaky in the way the essay tends to be. One would be ill-advised, therefore, to invoke White's as a blanket judgment of the essay, the essayist, or himself.

One would be similarly at risk in hastily branding and dismissing the essay as the most self-centered of literary forms. Self-conscious and self-aware, yes, but these qualities represent health, unlike self-centeredness. In more than one manner the essay moves outward, the essay and its writer connecting with the world, with otherness.

The position of the self in the essay is, in fact, rather problematic. The subject seems to be always "I," but the "I" can be present in a broad spectrum of possibilities, ranging from the assumption apparent in Sam Pickering's recent essays that anything of interest to him will be so for his readers, to Eliot's critical essays in which manner sometimes mirrors the argument for impersonality in poetry. In all cases, including John McPhee's journalistic essays, the form exploits the fact noted by Thoreau that, in writing generally, "it is, after all, always the first person that is speaking"; indeed, the essay takes its very nature from this fact, foregrounding what in other forms is only implicit or remains hidden. The "singular first person," to adopt Scott Russell Sanders's brilliant phrasing, speaks to us in essays; his nerves, his judgment are the crucible in which experience is tried and tested, balanced and weighed.[4] A genuinely unique, concrete, and particular angle of vision is manifest in all successful instances of the form. Even so, there remains the experience, *potentially* shareable by all of us, that the essayist assays, the general that exists alongside the particular. Despite all the blather about self-centeredness, the essayist never resembles the hack writer of Swift's *A Tale of a Tub*, in his isolated garret, indulging his imagination and imagining himself in possession of great truths—and writing "upon nothing."

Even Montaigne, taking his self as his supposedly exclusive subject, differs from Swift's spider who, in *The Battle of the Books*, spins out of his own entrails ("the guts of modern brains"), "feeding and engendering on itself," and so "turns all into excrement and venom" and thus "produces nothing at last, but flybane and a cobweb."[5] Even Montaigne's *raison d'être*, "Of Practice," derives from generalizable experience, includes a story replete with characters, and reflects on the relation between sleep and death; that particular essay does, indeed, look toward the private self's possible preparation for death, but Montaigne's anxious apology for his writing reflects an attention to and concern for the good opinion of his readers.

Although the essay might be mistaken as a solitary endeavor, an Other-ness attends it. At the very least, the essay normally assumes a reader, for the essayist is no monologist; he may sometimes appear indulgent, but never solipsistic or imprisoned in his own ego. William H. Gass has, without distortion, described the essay as "a commerce between friends." Noting the essayist's propensity for quoting—think of Hazlitt, especially, and Lamb—Gass has also written that "the essay convokes a community of writers.... It uses any and each and all of them like instruments in an orchestra. It both composes and conducts." Passages of texts are remembered, introduced, and shared—who quotes when merely indulging self-expression? Quotations often represent dialogue, but at the least they always reflect the presence—the reality—of an Other voice. Moreover, by quoting and citing, "the essay confirms the continuity, the contemporaneity, the reality of writing."[6] White implies as much when, acknowledging his own egoism, he reacts to Montaigne as predecessor and justification; implicitly, he is acknowledging his writing's participation in a tradition, in tradition.

In any case, the essay challenges this "I," this self, that is its basis. It focuses on the self, but without aggrandizing it. Instead, as Lopate has noted, "essayists are adept at interrogating their ignorance" and often indulge in "self-belittlement."[7] "Self-contradiction" is a staple of essays, and their writers characteristically adopt a stance so modest and humble as to appear self-effacing. One of the most striking and moving moments in an essay, for me, occurs in Nancy Mairs's "On Being a Cripple," included in the opening section (titled "Self") of *Plaintext*. Here she represents, with admirable honesty and candor, her own growth as a result of her debilitating disease (multiple sclerosis). What she dramatizes is a movement out of and away from self, a long and arduous process that had included self-pity. At the end, she writes the following, instancing an evolving gentleness that is also a development in sympathetic understanding reflective of self-centeredness's opposite:

> The absence of a cure often makes MS patients bitter toward their doctors. Doctors are, after all, the priests of modern society, the new shamans, whose business is to heal, and many an MS patient roves from one to another, searching for the "good" doctor who

will make him well. Doctors too think of themselves as healers, and
for this reason many have trouble dealing with MS patients, whose
disease in its intransigence defeats their aims and mocks their skills.
Too few doctors, it is true, treat their patients as whole human
beings, but the reverse is also true. I have always tried to be gentle
with my doctors, who often have more at stake in terms of ego than
I do. I may be frustrated, maddened, depressed by the incurability
of my disease, but I am not diminished by it, and they are. When
I push myself up from my seat in the waiting room and stumble
toward them, I incarnate the limitation of their powers. The least I
can do is refuse to press on their tenderest spots.[8]

Writing here, (in) this essay, Mairs embodies devotion to the situation of others.

Consider, too, Zora Neale Hurston's "How It Feels to Be Colored Me," an altogether different kind of essay, written without, I would say, gentleness but evincing transcendence of any self-pity or self-indulgence to which, as an African American, she might be tempted. There is pride, but it is entirely justified, and I can only applaud it, for it never veers toward arrogance. The tone is indeed remarkable—complex and supple, composed and not bitter, even if anger is just below the surface:

Someone is always at my elbow reminding me that I am the granddaughter of slaves. It fails to register depression with me. Slavery is sixty years in the past. The operation was successful and the patient is doing well, thank you. The terrible struggle that made me an American out of a potential slave said "On the line!" The Reconstruction said "Get set!"; and the generation before said "Go!" I am off to a flying start and I must not halt in the stretch to look behind and weep. Slavery is the price I paid for civilization, and the choice was not with me. It is a bully adventure and worth all that I have paid through my ancestors for it. No one on earth ever had a greater chance for glory. The world to be won and nothing to be lost. It is thrilling to think—to know that for any act of mine, I shall get twice as much praise or twice as much blame. It is quite exciting to hold the center of the national stage, with the spectators not knowing whether to laugh or to weep.[9]

Hurston immediately adds a consideration of "the other"; the tone here is edgier, and you feel the difference that she will exploit in the brilliant description later in the essay of her and a white friend at a Harlem cabaret: "The position of my white neighbor is much more difficult. No brown specter pulls up a chair beside me when I sit down to eat. No dark ghost thumps its leg against mine in bed. The game of keeping what one has is never so exciting as the game of getting."[10] Hardly self-effacing or unassuming, Hurston embodies a complexity of response that is nevertheless balanced with composure. It is remarkable the way that balance exists despite obvious tension—perhaps the latter is responsible for the former.

More commonly, essayists appear self-deprecating: for instance, Richard Selzer opening "A Worm from My Notebook": "Were I a professor of the art of writing...."[11] Selzer, who taught writing as well as surgery at Yale and who writes elsewhere of the positive relation between pen and scalpel, made "An Absence of Windows" a deflation of the medical practitioner's ego. White was, of course, a master of the pose: a layman, an amateur, a man common enough except for certain skills in putting words down on paper, a craftsman in that regard and an artisan—but not an artist or some God-like figure! The character fits, a mantle essayists find comfortable, descended as it is from Montaigne. Lopate says finely: "In exchange for lack of stature or power in the world, the personal essayist claims unique access to the small, humble things in life."[12] Theodor Adorno has even said that the essay "revolts above all against the doctrine—deeply rooted since Plato—that the changing and ephemeral is unworthy of philosophy, against the ancient injustice toward the transitory." Echoing Robert Louis Stevenson, Adorno distinguishes the essay from "the violence of dogma," for the essayist knows no such certainty nor reveals the arrogance of the dogmatist.[13] Sam Pickering is, perhaps, the extreme version of contemporary antidogmatists and self-deprecators (although, at times, he gets astride his high horse in proclaiming his cultural conservatism).

As to self-correction, it is an altogether more demanding task to accomplish. What Ezra Pound translated as Confucius's starting-point is viable—and difficult: you look into your own heart, honestly, clearly, and steadfastly. I think White does that in "Death of a Pig" and reveals, as a result, some not entirely attractive facets of himself. Elsewhere I discuss this essay in detail, but for now I would add that, even as he represents himself as self-concerned and very much like the essayist as he depicted him in the foreword to the 1977 *Essays*, White shows more darkness than he intended. This essay functions, I suggest, somewhat in the way Browning's dramatic monologues do, although these poems are spoken by a character distinct from the author: the speaker unwittingly reveals parts of himself he would surely prefer not to. In "Death of a Pig" the reader sees more than White does, and he, of course, sees quite a lot, dramatizing his own fears and failures.

THE MOST SELF-CENTERED OF FORMS?

As it has developed since the retired mayor of Bordeaux sat down in 1580 to map himself, the essay has existed somewhere on a line between the two sturdy poles of inner and outer, experience and meaning, "I" and "the world." In Montaigne the scales tip toward the self, whereas Bacon appears often as a counterbalance, certainly very different in texture and attention. Some would be inclined to say that the Englishman goes too far in the opposite direction, his essays formal, prescriptive, and didactic. I view them as trials, attempts to find the way in a new mode of expression. Montaigne did not, once and for all, with one taking-up of his pen, determine the force and direction of this new form, nor did Bacon a few years later. Rather, they may be seen as the ends of the spectrum on which the essay has always played. Regarded in this way, the essay can be said to lurch toward the article if Montaigne's manner is too much ignored, toward the memoir, perhaps a mere self-expression, if Bacon's is neglected.

This very tension in the evolution of the essay is sometimes apparent in a given writing, most notably perhaps Thoreau's *Walden*. The book begins by serving notice on the reader that there will be no downplaying here of "the I," Thoreau foregrounding the fact that "the first person is speaking." And indeed, Thoreau figures more prominently as the seat of attention early on than later; a marked change appears as he moves through the book, a collection of closely related essays. Lawrence Buell puts it this way, in his magisterial recent book, *The Environmental Imagination*: as some other "nature writers" before him had done, Thoreau managed to "cultivate a nonegoistic, ecocentric sensibility toward which [he] had to grope his way laboriously, as he slowly managed to get down on paper how much more being at Walden meant to him than an experiment in economic self-sufficiency, how much more was entailed in fathoming Walden than merely thinking about what it meant to him."[14] In the course of things, according to Buell, an evolution occurred, marked by a "relinquishment" of that celebrated "I" and the ascendancy of words and notions referring to the outer world of Walden, pond(s), "and the various nominal and adjectival forms of 'wild.'"[15] Although no "eradication" of ego occurs, there is "suspension of ego to the point of feeling the environment to be at least as worthy of attention as oneself and of experiencing oneself as situated among many interacting presences." In the end, Buell concludes, the essays that constitute *Walden* represent neither the disappearance nor the self-assertion of the author or his persona, this text being neither a lyric nor a scientific report. The kind of balance, with its acceptance of tension, that Buell locates in Thoreau's essays here matches that that results from the bringing together of Montaigne and Bacon: "The effect," he writes,

> on the perceiving self, as I see it, is not primarily to fulfill it, to negate it, or even to complicate it, although all of these may seem to happen. Rather the effect is most fundamentally to raise the question of the validity of the self as the primary focalizing device for both writer and reader: to make me wonder, for instance, whether the self is as interesting an object of study as we supposed, whether the world would become more interesting if we could see it from the perspective of a wolf, a sparrow, a river, a stone. This approach to subjectivity makes apparent that the "I" has no greater claims to being the main subject than the chickens, the chopped corn, the mice, the snake, and the phoebes—who are somehow also interwoven with me.[16]

A powerful, and some would say extreme, statement of environmental consciousness, this position marks a significant departure from the exploration, cultivation, and celebration of subjectivity that Montaigne enacted and bequeathed to us. Without necessarily agreeing with all points and directions here, I find this reading of *Walden* extremely suggestive for consideration of the essay, the form that nature writing too has traditionally espoused.

AS HAPPENS in *Walden*, so too the development of the essay from Montaigne to Bacon and on to Johnson, Hazlitt, Lamb, Arnold, Woolf, Orwell, and White: "the world" asserts itself, challenging in individual instances the primacy of self, sometimes winning, sometimes losing. The history of the essay tells the story of this struggle, this back-and-forth effort toward balance of strong and competing forces. Tension lies at the heart of that history.

In so many ways, Hilaire Belloc's essay "The Mowing of a Field" proves unavoidable, even exemplary as I have already hinted. To appreciate how it sheds light on the matters now before us, consider first how Romantic writing differs from it, reveling in the self's primacy. In Wordsworth, whose Preface to *Lyrical Ballads* often reads like an apology for the essay and whose revolutionary poems are lyrical essays in verse, the self may be called the principal "focalizing device" and more; indeed, the self is the object of study as it perceives and responds (elsewhere) to ten thousand daffodils. Thus when, in "Resolution and Independence," Wordsworth comes upon an old leech-gatherer he is so locked inside his own response that he barely attends to the man or what he is saying (occasioning Lewis Carroll's parody in "The White Knight's Song"). So it is, too, that

Wordsworth concludes his greatest poem *The Prelude*, subtitled *Growth of a Poet's Mind—An Autobiographical Poem*, with this assertion:

> ... the mind of Man becomes
> A thousand times more beautiful than the earth
> On which he dwells, above this frame of things
> (Which 'mid all revolutions in the hopes
> And fears of men, doth still remain unchanged)
> In beauty exalted, as it is itself
> Of quality and fabric more divine. (14.448–54)[17]

In prose, Hazlitt does not go so far, but clearly one of his greatest and most frequently anthologized essays, "On Going a Journey," reflects the same Romantic proclivity. The interest lies in the self who goes walking alone, rather than in people or places encountered; consequently, experience matters mainly insofar as it relates to that perceiving self, whose habits are then scrutinized and brought into the province of the association of ideas.

By the time we reach Belloc, the Romantic revolution has run its course, and now a backlash can be felt, including "The Mowing of a Field," which roundly rejects the Wordsworthianism or Romanticism of "the bad or young or untaught mower without tradition, the mower Promethean, the mower original and contemptuous of the past." Belloc's essay itself participates alongside a tradition of "mower poems" from the Renaissance (notably including work by Marvell). The scene in the essay—a farm, isolated, in the south of England, far from "the dry bones of commerce, avarice and method and need" that the residents there find "odious"—is as pastoral as any in Wordsworth a hundred years before, but the texture of perception, response, and focus is quite different.[18] Of primary interest is not Belloc's mind but at once the quality of his response and "the world" he experiences. Natural description early on, which draws us in and always attracts students, soon gives way to accounts of the arts of sharpening the scythe and thence of mowing, interspersed with reflections that move outward to greater and greater implications of the ways we do seemingly minor acts. "The world is too much with us," lamented Wordsworth, and Belloc too retires, as did Montaigne before either of them, from its "getting and spending." But Belloc does so temporarily, for refreshment, and rather than forsake it, works out alternatives. Rather than escape, his strong cultural criticism is aimed at recognition, judgment, and change.

In the south of England, that world beyond the Valley is always impinging. We encounter it in the brief story of the hasty and greedy "London man," "a man in a motor-car, a man in a fur coat, a man of few words," who, failing to observe the necessary rituals and heedless of custom and tradition, gets his deserved comeuppance. Not quite such a contrast, but important nevertheless, is the irruption onto this placid scene of an Other, a character, a member of "that dark silent race," perhaps Iberian or Celtic at root, who seeks employ.[19] Belloc thus opens up and out, the self developed but not diminished—on the contrary, this receptivity and openness validates the self. Indirections find directions out, as Polonius allowed.

With respect to the essay, the differences we are noting may be referred to the distinction between the personal and the familiar forms. Lopate, we recall, begins by recognizing that difference but soon ends in a morass of virtual interchangeability. The need persists to distinguish, and the basis for doing so lies before us. Not surprisingly, given the "me-culture" in which we find ourselves, constructed on the quicksand of self-esteem, self-assertion, and self-validation, the "personal" essay reigns supreme, the "familiar" rarely mentioned. At some historical moments one ascends at the expense of the other, and now you would be hard-pressed to find any essays but Joseph Epstein's promoted as familiar.

The difference between personal and familiar essays resembles that between Bacon and Montaigne, although we need be careful, for these are also shifting sands. Take a look at Bacon's essays: every one of them begins with the tiny but telling preposition "of." Many of Montaigne's do as well. The difference between the familiar essay and the personal resides, however subtly and slightly, in the degree to which the scales tip away from the perceiving self and toward the perceived world. Neither the familiar nor the personal essay should be confused with the memoir. Unlike the memoir, in both essay forms there is a generalizable point toward which the whole moves; and as to the self, as Lopate has said, "The trick is to realize that one is not important, except insofar as one's example can serve to elucidate a more widespread human trait and make readers feel a little less lonely and freakish."[20] The familiar form of the essay edges more than the personal toward the meaning the writer extracts from experience. Because the focus rests "on" books or morality or friendship, self-consciousness is tempered and the temptation toward self-centeredness challenged.

We have only begun to tap the surface of these complex and important issues, and so in the following chapter I shall return to them in a different and somewhat larger context.

ASSAYING EXPERIENCE
TIME, MEANING, AND THE ESSAY

How to spend our time; where to go; who to be . . .

Paying attention, working the mind on whatever moves into its ambit—these are nothing other than ways of using our time and, as such, they speak to our moment-by-moment formation as human selves: what to do, who to be. You are what you do with your time. The responsiveness that is, in one sense, our aesthetic posture belongs inextricably and most deeply to our moral life.
Lydia Fakundiny, *The Art of the Essay*

"IT'S ABOUT TIME" at once describes the drive of the essay, its essential direction if you will, and points to the revival, at last, of this venerable form after decades of desuetude. News of its death, proclaimed by Joseph Wood Krutch in 1951 and born of curricular and popular neglect alike, proved greatly exaggerated. The essay began a remarkable comeback some twenty years ago and now is granted, if somewhat grudgingly, status as "the fourth genre." "Ours is the age of the essay," one editor even touted some time ago.[1] Although no doubt self-interested, Scott Russell Sanders was surely right in declaring that, while "we do not have anyone to rival Emerson or Thoreau," or, I would add, White or Woolf or Orwell, "in sheer quantity of first-rate work our time stands comparison with any period since the heyday of the form in the mid-nineteenth century."[2]

The essay has a certain timeliness that Sanders judges to be the reason why so many writers have taken up "this risky form" and why so many readers ("to judge by the statistics of book and magazine publication") are embracing it. "In this era of prepackaged thought," he writes in "The Singular First Person," "the essay is the closest thing we have, on paper, to a record of the individual mind at work and play. It is an amateur's raid in a world of specialists." This is well said, as is the subsequent proclamation *cum* lament that "The essay is a haven for the private, idiosyncratic voice in an era of anonymous babble."[3] I may think that Sanders misses the tension and the delicate balance that marks the essay's relation to the private and the public, the individual and tradition, but I agree that it represents a necessary if usually implicit criticism of contemporary culture and the primacy that culture places on impersonalism (of sorts). Social commentators may deplore our anonymity, estrangement, and loss of individuality, but most of us, meanwhile, have no time to ponder abstractions, reflect on ideas, or pause to consider what makes life worth living. "The art of living" may have exercised Epictetus, Montaigne, and E. B. White, but we, today, are too busy with instant and constant communication and the busyness of business. The business of living—or, rather, of surviving and succeeding, of getting and spending (and so, "laying waste our powers," said Wordsworth)—has long since replaced the art of living for too many of us.

In this frenetic pace, we have lost something necessary and good. Gained, to be sure, is efficiency, the great god whom we daily worship: get in, get out, get on with it, the quicker the better. Polonius appears but a fool when he advises, "By indirections, find directions out." Sacrificing care and craft and at the mercy of the clock, we have no time to reflect. To pause, to reflect—these mean waywardness, and our way is strict, linear, straightforward: panic attends detour, delay, or misstep. We rush into sex, into marriage, and into divorce, although souls as well as bodies require time to become attuned to each other, at-oned. Rape names our haste in laying waste nature and in conquering each other.

"Fair seed-time needs the soul," said Wordsworth on the brink of the Industrial Revolution, moved too deeply for tears by recognition not only of what was to come but also of what was already happening. In the Preface to *Lyrical Ballads*, a manifesto of the Romantic reaction, Wordsworth decried "this degrading thirst after outrageous stimulation" that took men (and women too) away from cultivation and refinement of sensibility: "a craving for extraordinary incident, which the rapid communication of intelligence hourly gratifies." He called, and no wonder, his and Coleridge's poems "short essays," offering them as part of "the present outcry against the triviality and meanness, both of thought and language." He directed his effort, accordingly, toward "incidents and situations from common life," his eye constant on "the essential passions of the heart."[4] Time becomes the Romantic object as well as subject, time the destroyer a frequent theme and a characteristic lament of poets like Wordsworth.

Inheritors of the Romantic tradition, we would likely agree that time is a gigantic, unavoidable wreckage—if we but took the time to reflect on it. Of course, we do not because we are too busy, busy beyond need and eager to avoid truth, especially that which signals our mortality. I say "we" fairly confidently, for I acknowledge my own failings and pusillanimity as I come armed with the well-rehearsed diagnoses of contemporary culture, too familiar to require elaboration or merit citation. The point remains distressingly simple: efficiency precludes reflection, meditation, contemplation, or any breach of its ruthless straightforward march. In this situation, the wayward, protean essay very nearly died ignominiously.

It persisted, fortunately, and now appears to have prevailed. Its respect for time, I believe, is more important—certainly more salutary—than its touted individualism. As something of a ramble or saunter, the essay takes its time, in no hurry, unlike its opposite, "that awful object," the professional article that, knowing only logic and proceeding in *a priori* fashion, marches directly and smartly to its foreseen conclusion, suffering no digression or wavering along its straight and narrow path. While the essay is by no means formless, it follows no prescribed path, its form immanent, a matter of each instance's purposive movement. There is nothing to prevent digression, to prevent taking a tangent that suddenly appears attractive, because the apparent digression contributes.

Opposed to systems and systematizing and wary of *a priori* thinking, the essay, a product of the Renaissance and a child of the age of exploration and discovery, prizes as it foregrounds experience. As it maps the territory of the self, the essay details the particulars of everyday life, attuned, like Wordsworth and like Dutch genre painting, to the quite mundane and quotidian: taking a walk, mowing a field, observing a moth dying, contemplating a piece of chalk. The wonder is not that art can be made of such ordinary stuff, but that we should expect it to be found anywhere else. "Were I a professor of the art of writing," has written Richard Selzer, who was just that as well as a surgeon, "I would coax my students to eschew all great and noble concepts. . . . There are no 'great' subjects for the creative writer; there are only the singular details of a single human life."[5] And of course, there are also the familiar objects and "uneventful events" that join to create the living texture of life, its coloration, the seasoning that (in at least this sense) distinguishes it.

Essays differ from purely autobiographical writing in the degree to which they point to experience, not merely representing it and detailing it in both its particularity and its ordinariness, but also in deriving meaning from it. Meaning thus marks the essay as well as, and as much as, experience. In the essay, experience is weighed and assayed for its value and meaning, which derive from reflection, meditation, or contemplation. Autobiographical writing absent reflection and such attempts to derive meaning is not essayistic.

In providing reflection, essays remind us of the urgency to slow down and savor experience, certainly, but also to measure and weigh it, to try it and test it. Understood this way, reflection comprises an essential aspect of our ordinary living, part of the whole rather than addendum or supplement, and an aspect without which our lives are sorely diminished. As the point where meaning and experience cross, the essay is the place where, it is legitimate to say, time and the timeless meet. Essays, I repeat, offer a generalizable point that distinguishes them from other sorts of autobiographical expression. That point is the contact, however brief, with the timeless amidst the essay's full engagement with the flux of ordinary existence. In this way, the essay is incarnational in structure.

Although concern with time marks the essay from its beginnings in Montaigne—think of his reflections on death and preparations for it in "On Practice"—full engagement with it may come only in the magnificent essays of E. B. White. In work after work, White reflects on time, its putative circular nature, its relation with space: for example, the justly famous and revered "The Ring of Time," the oft-reprinted "Death of a Pig," and "What Do Our Hearts Treasure?" as well as such laments for a lost time as "Once More to the Lake" and "Coon Tree." White would no doubt scoff at my notion that his work *incarnates* anything, self-described as a "second-class citizen." Time, I am sure, he would grant as among any essayist's favorite bag of themes, but the notion of his "little" essays as "incarnating" would arouse his legendary Yankee skepticism. Embracing the essay, White understood, without necessarily being fully conscious of the implications and however inchoately, how the timeless intersects time, giving experience its meaning—the work of the essayist reflecting, meditating, sometimes contemplating what he or she has gone through, read, and heard about.

Essaying, then, as assaying: trying, testing, weighing, sifting for gold amidst so much pyrite.

THE ESSAY had its heyday in the nineteenth century, in England and America alike. No wonder, since Romanticism and the essay seem veritable soul mates, Wordsworth himself defending the one and implying the other in the Preface to *Lyrical Ballads*, celebrating both the author's own expressiveness and his reflections. In the process—although it has never been much noticed—he refers to his and Coleridge's included poems as "short essays." The Preface may, in fact, be read as a defense of the essay as of the lyrical poem, awaiting T. S. Eliot's stricture and reversal 125 years later. (In *Dreamthorp*, in the 1850s, Alexander Smith implicitly linked the lyric and the essay in describing the latter according to the writer's "mood.")[6]

Of course, long before Eliot, Keats objected to Wordsworth and such Romanticism, reviling him as "the wordsworthian or egotistical sublime" and decrying the way, so he claimed, his fellow-Romantic "bullie[s]" us "into a certain Philosophy engendered in the whims of an Egotist—Every man has his speculations, but every man does not brood and peacock over them till he makes a false coinage and deceives himself."[7] Not so "the father" of the essay, whose "speculations" and reflections never seem "peacocked" or lorded over us or merely self-expressive. Something happens in Montaigne—and in Hazlitt, Arnold, Thoreau, E. B. White, Cynthia Ozick, Richard Selzer, and Scott Russell Sanders—that differs from Wordsworth's manifesto for Romantic poetry. That the aforementioned essayists write in prose—very good prose, with definite elements and virtues of poetry included—has something to do with it. Anne Carson notes it in a recent interview, discussing her collection of poems *The Beauty of the Husband*, presented as "a fictional essay": "To me, calling it an essay means that it's not just a story but reflection on that story, which is also a way of making it less personal or not only personal."[8] This kind of essay, traditionally called familiar, while sharing characteristics of the lyrical and self-expressive that Wordsworth extols, goes beyond, moving from described event and narrated action toward the derivation of its significance and meaning. "Essay" means attempt, trial, but it also refers, I have been insisting, to that weighing that its not-so-secret self denotes as "assay."

Wordsworth, however, remains difficult to challenge, impossible to dismiss, being prescient as well as having been proven right on so many accounts. What I am most concerned with here is his continuing relevance, and I mean specifically not so much his diagnosis of cultural and psychological disintegration as his insight into the plague of "outrageous stimulation" and its disastrous effects. Our cravings grow daily more sordid and crude, self-control long since banished.

Wordsworth spoke from conviction, insisting that we cultivate the capacity for discrimination while resisting the forces that blunt our inherent and trainable powers. Although his analysis focuses on the consequences of the mind, rather than, as did his fellow Romantic Robert Burns, the heart, its acuity behooves our heed: "the human mind," writes Wordsworth in this key passage, is capable of being excited without the application of gross and violent stimulants; and he must have a very faint perception of its beauty and dignity who does not know this, and who does not further know, that one being is elevated above another, in proportion as he possesses this capability. It has therefore appeared to me, that the endeavour to produce or enlarge this capability is one of the best services in which, at any period, a Writer can be engaged; but this service, excellent at all times, is especially so at the present day. For a multitude of causes, unknown to former times, are now acting with a combined force to blunt the discriminating powers of the mind, and, unfitting it for all voluntary exertion, to reduce it to a state of almost savage torpor.... When I think upon this degrading thirst after outrageous stimulation, I am almost ashamed to have spoken of the feeble endeavour made in these volumes to counteract it; and, reflecting upon the magnitude of the general evil, I should be oppressed with no dishonourable melancholy, had I not a deep impression of certain inherent and indestructible qualities of the human mind, and likewise of certain powers in the great and permanent objects that act upon it, which are equally inherent and indestructible; and were there not further added to this impression a belief, that the time is approaching when the evil will be systematically opposed, by men of greater powers, and with far more distinguished success.[9]

At the very least, Wordsworth's "belief" has proven much too sanguine. The extent of the problem appears in the difficulty we now have—as my students demonstrate—in even hearing Wordsworth. Thanks, no doubt, to "sound bites" and perhaps this demon computer, we seem increasingly unable to "process" long and thoughtful sentences. Wordsworth's, of course, can't be swallowed whole; they require time and respect, for you must take them in controlled measure and digest them.

I think naturally of Wordsworth's friend Hazlitt, arguably the greatest of all nineteenth-century British essayists. "On Going a Journey," a veritable allegory of essaying, incarnates the values whose passing Wordsworth decries: it moves ever so slowly, like life in the Lake District—the opening paragraph consumes three full pages—in no hurry whatsoever, digressing to observe and reflect, and ending up where serendipity, Grace, or the writing's own will delivers the writer. Modern and postmodern readers, marching to an entirely different drummer, unfortunately greet this essay with a combination of dismay and impatience. What, sadly, they miss or mistake is that this pedestrian subject is treated in no pedestrian way. What you do, what you see, how you respond makes all the difference—the extraordinary blooms in the ordinary for all with eyes to see with (Pound's way of describing literature's power). Hazlitt calls to the reader to respond in the spirit of the author—which Pope identified as the art of reading. As Hazlitt slows down to observe, reflect, and appreciate, so must the reader. Give walking, give reading, a chance, seems to be the point of the essay, Hazlitt's and all those others comprising "the fourth genre." Take a line out for a walk, averred the artist Paul Klee, an apt description of the essayist's work.

That "hair shirt of a man," Henry David Thoreau, sauntered to a drummer that few others have ever taken the time to listen to. As a result, he penned great essays such as "Walking" (which opens with an excursion around "sauntering," related, he surmises, to *sans terre*) and those that make up *Walden*. Seeking a life of "simplicity and independence," in early 1845 Thoreau left Concord, "borrowed an axe and went down to the woods by Walden Pond." "My purpose in going to Walden Pond," he wrote, "was not to live cheaply nor to live dearly there, but to transact some private business with the fewest obstacles," intent on living "simply and wisely; as the pursuits of the simpler nations are still the sports of the more artificial."[10] In an eloquent and ringing passage in the second essay in *Walden*, "Where I Lived, and What I Lived For," Thoreau explains:

> I went to the woods because I wished to live deliberately, to front only the essential facts of life, and see if I could not learn what it had to teach, and not, when I came to die, discover that I had not lived. I did not wish to live what was not life, living is so dear; nor did I wish to practice resignation, unless it was quite necessary. I wanted to live deep and suck out all the marrow of life, to live so sturdily and Spartan-like as to put to rout all that was not life, to cut a broad swath and shave close, to drive life into a corner, and reduce it to its lowest terms, and, if it proved to be mean, why then to get the whole and genuine meanness of it, and publish its meanness to the world; or if it were sublime, to know it by experience, and be able to give a true account of it in my next excursion.[11]

What Thoreau flees from is as important as what he confronts, the antithesis always just below the surface of these meticulous accounts of musquatch and bean fields, warring ants and springing hillside. The Fitchburg Railroad is the most brutal encroachment upon the pastoral landscape whose sounds and shapes, beauty and ministrations Thoreau urges us to heed—and teaches us to read ("Reading," we remember, is *Walden*'s third essay). "Let us spend one day as deliberately as Nature, and not be thrown off the track by every nutshell and mosquito's wing that falls on the rails." Just such fripperies derail and wreck, as well as wrack, us: "Our life is frittered away by detail," Thoreau laments, juxtaposing it with the cry "Simplicity, simplicity, simplicity."[12] That cry E. B. White took to heart, adopting Thoreau's notion of the art of writing as of the art of living, and in the event coauthoring the magnificent "little book" *Elements of Style* as well as crafting such magisterial essays as his centennial tribute to *Walden*, "A Slight Sound at Evening."

Thoreau's self-styled "experiment" and the masterpiece it spawned are, in every sense, an essay, a genuine trial upon life and meaning that is also a deeply reflective assaying. White says that "It restored me to health." As he writes memorably of *Walden* as like "an invitation to life's dance," White acknowledges its author's "two powerful and opposing drives—the desire to enjoy the world (and not be derailed by a mosquito wing) and the urge to set the world straight."[13] He himself writes in the spirit of Thoreau, not at all imitating him or slavishly following him (which would fly in the face of *Walden*'s paean to independence), but so flooded by his writing and sympathetically engaged with the heart and mind that he follows Pope's sage advice. Perhaps hearkening to the "outrageous stimulation" so much greater in 1954 than in 1854 (although not nearly so craven and dehumanizing as now) White observes:

> I doubt that Thoreau would be thrown off balance by the fantastic sights and sounds of the twentieth century. . . . Everywhere he would observe, in new shapes and sizes, the old predicaments and follies of men—the desperation, the impedimenta, the meanness—along with the visible capacity for elevation of the mind and soul. "This curious world which we inhabit is more wonderful than it is

convenient; more beautiful than it is useful; it is more to be admired and enjoyed than used." He would see that today ten thousand engineers are busy making sure that the world shall be convenient even if it is destroyed in the process, and others are determined to increase its usefulness even though its beauty is lost somewhere along the way.[14]

Elsewhere White pursues these asseverations against "progress" while attending closely to the dazzling light of the extraordinary he finds in Maine and Florida and New York among the quite ordinary: a young circus performer among the sibilants of the South and its querulous quest to stop time, a coon descending a tree tail-first, his own troubled involvement in the death of a not-so-simple pig. In these lustrous little stories, as moving as eloquent, we watch White read (sometimes watching Thoreau read) amidst persistence and permanence and signs of a moral order he never identifies nor perhaps understands as such.

In a series of essays now comprising several collections, Scott Russell Sanders has, for some twenty years, been writing of just the simplicity that Wordsworth, Thoreau, and White celebrate. "Speaking a Word for Nature," gathered with "The Singular First Person" and thirteen other essays in *Secrets of the Universe: Scenes from the Journey Home*, includes a trenchant critique of the shallowness and insipidity of contemporary fiction. Sanders's particular concern lies with nature and the way our best writers have sought "to understand our life as continuous with the life of nature; they project 'the little human morality play' against the 'wilderness raging round.'" From this perspective Sanders takes to task Bobbie Ann Mason, in whose *Shiloh and Other Stories* "nature supplies an occasional metaphor to illustrate a character's dilemma—a tulip tree cut down when it was about to bloom, a rabbit with crushed legs on the highway—exactly as Kmart and Cat Chow and the Phil Donohue Show supply analogues."[15] Sanders proceeds, Thoreauvian at heart, to these telling remarks that show just how much more of our sensibility has been deadened since Wordsworth decried "the accumulation of men in cities," the effects of the media, and the consequences of indulging sentimental and extravagant literature:

> That a deep awareness of nature has been largely excluded from "mainstream" fiction is a measure of the narrowing and trivialization of that fashionable current. It is also, of course, and more dangerously, a measure of a shared blindness in the culture at large. Not long ago, while camping in the Great Smoky Mountains, I had a nightmare glimpse of the modern reader. It was late one afternoon in May, the air sweet and mild. I left my tent and crossed the parking lot of the campground on my way to a cliff, where I planned to sit with my legs dangling over the brink and stare out across the westward mountains at the sunset. Already the sky was throbbing with color and the birds were settling down for their evening song. The wind smelled of pines. Near the center of the parking lot, as far as possible from the encircling trees, a huge camping van squatted. There were chocks under the tires, but the motor was running. The air-conditioner gave a high frantic squeal. The van had enough windows for a hothouse, but every one was curtained, even the windshield. Lights glowed around the edges and threw yellow slashes onto the blacktop. What could keep the passengers shut up inside that box on such an afternoon, in such a place? Passing by, I saw through a gap in the curtains a family clustered in front of a

television as if in front of a glowing hearth, and I heard the unmistakable banshee cry of Tarzan, King of the Apes.[16]

Sanders's enemy, and that of all great writers, is "the superficial consciousness of an age," to which (a certain kind of) art contributes importantly. But "durable art, art that matters," writes Sanders, is the product of writers—here he cites Cervantes, Melville, Faulkner, and García Márquez—who "quarreled with the dominant ways of seeing, and in that quarreling with the actual they enlarged our vision of the possible"[17]—as E. B. White does in "Coon Tree," "A Report in January," and "The Winter of the Great Snows" and as Sanders does here. His is a voice we ignore at our peril—although we have to strain to hear it above the din of engines, so-called music, and the declarations of ideologues making a mockery of our institutions as they seek to draw all into the only center they know, the vortex of Self.

Into this situation, much exacerbated now, saunters the essay, breathing quietly and speaking softly and eloquently: not a voice crying in the wilderness but one witnessing to values trampled under the iron boot of commerce, ideology, and all forms of exclusion and totalitarianism. Inherently critical, the essay speaks, even when it seems merely quaint and nostalgic, for values alternative to those dominating. It does indeed offer a way of seeing, helping to clear the vision of cultural detritus and the desires of a rapacious selfhood.

To the "degrading thirst after outrageous stimulation," the essay opposes itself, taking a stand on several fronts. I am talking here of the nature of this venerable and protean form, rather than the particularities of individual examples of that art. I offer the following as some specific ways in which the essay as form addresses the situation that Wordsworth identified and that looms now as one of our greatest cultural challenges.

I know of no more accurate representation of this address than Hilaire Belloc's seemingly quaint but actually sophisticated and prescient "The Mowing of a Field," from near the beginning of the last century. The scene is pastoral: the essayist's return home to the south of England, an Archimedean point, an "unwobbling pivot," in early June. There, in the most modest of contexts, Belloc reflects on huge topics, to which mowing leads him as if the product of the Grace he never mentions (but implicitly acknowledges here and explicitly elsewhere). After panegyrics on traditional ways of doing things—sharpening the scythe, mowing—that he opposes to Prometheanism and its contemptuousness of the past, Belloc draws to a close this essay on tradition and the individual talent with a story of labor and commerce worthy of E. B. White and Henry David Thoreau (I quoted this earlier). Haste bespeaks both greed and violence, according to Belloc, whose saunter of mind here reflects the antidote to recklessness: "The Mowing of a Field" incarnates the heart heeled—and healed.

Belloc embodies what he advocates, his essay an instance of the desired alternative: against haste, greed, and violence he opposes, simply, independently, slowing down, taking your time. From experience—both teaching and writing the essay—I bear witness that slowing down is key. It is what the essay does: what it teaches and what is required for achievement in the form.

After decades of struggling with my writing—never my strong suit, the result of an expressive nature reined in and very nearly overwhelmed by the different exclusions and confinements of journalism and graduate study in English—I learned, late, the greatest lesson of my life about writing. It came via a rejection, this one from a well-known editor of an important publishing house, to whom I had submitted a book of autobiographical essays bearing the grand Emersonian title *Essaying to Be*. Her response was brief but polite: the manuscript was "interesting," but the story of my own struggles to write was "not quite enough" to "hang a book on." Still, she said, "You write well, and are most effective when you slow down sufficiently to allow your details to accumulate weight." More encouraged than otherwise—than perhaps I should have been—I took another look at my writing, comparing passages I had cobbled with some in essayists I admire. I saw, finally, what I had never seen before: in my newspaper writing and my scholarship and criticism alike, I had *rushed*, eager and anxious for the finish line. I was being driven by the task of getting done, meeting the morning deadline at the Greenville *Piedmont*, getting my papers in on time for seminars on Swift and Pope and on critical theory. Hostage now to a thesis as I had been to "the news" and its point, I was committed to a writing predicated on a certain logical clarity that would brook no digressing or pausing as "the worst of sinning" (as Lord Byron put it in *Don Juan*). My writing really did march, one eye on the clock, the other on the finish line. I was enslaved to efficiency, if not one of those masses of men that Thoreau regrets living "lives of quiet desperation," still, less oppressed, a prisoner of time management who had lost his independence and any feeling or respect for simplicity.

I hope and need to clarify that I am not now advocating something as trite and banal as "stopping to smell the roses" (although one profits from doing so) or as jejune as "letting it all hang out," throwing form and shape to the winds. What the aforementioned editor taught me, and what examination of effective essays confirms, is quite different: writing essays requires a change of pace—and of heart. Writing that someone else wants to read, writing that is respectful of its subject(s), entails noting and representing particulars, fleshing out scenes and characters with the details that they deserve and that readers need in order to participate in the "story." You simply have to take the time to observe and to see and absorb and then to pass along the full picture, rather than, as we teach in far too many writing classes, to come quickly to the point. The essay is not a pointed—*à-pic*—form; it is—to use an inelegant phrase—process- rather than product-oriented. "Somewhere" the essay "contains a point which is its real center," but as Edward Hoagland adds, that "point couldn't be uttered in fewer words than the essayist has used." Not so the article, with its "systematized outline of ideas" and its thesis directly and efficiently announced in the very first paragraph, thus obviating the possibility of diversion, digression, and discovery alike.[18] Whereas the article—newspaper or professional/academic—thus confines, the essay, as inclusive as it is processual, opens up and out, welcoming, capacious, and generous.

In addition to careful and detailed observation and representation, the essay takes the time, first, to notice and record and then, second, to weigh, or assay, what has been mined for its worth and value. We tend to overlook or at least minimize this crucial fact of assaying, in our haste to define the form as trial or attempt. The essay, I preach to my classes, is the crucible in which personal experience is tried and tested, weighed and judged for its meaning and significance. In Anne Carson's words again, an essay is "not just a story but a reflection on that story, which is also a way of making it less personal or not only personal."

Reflecting, the essayist cannot merely tell us *that* but also show us *how* and *why*. At the beginning of my courses on the essay, students show the ill effects of the usual instruction in writing, even when writing personally (for a change), in greedy haste and rushing through. A recent attempt by a junior is a case in point: she took the well-known—I don't say "hackneyed"—topic of the Kansas basketball tradition, committing a few paragraphs to her youthful exposure to television and family influence, her developing commitment in high school, and her barely expressible joy upon enrolling as a Jayhawk. There was nothing generalizable in the piece, and no weighing of her desire or her delight. This writing gave the reader next to nothing particular and fleshed out, nothing for even the interested reader to see and feel; nor did it attempt to show how it feels to be such a rabid Jayhawk fan. The author merely kept repeating that she is a fan, in the form of a narrative of her journey to the Land of Oz and hoops and Roy-mania (this before, of course, Coach Roy Williams bolted back to UNC)—all this in barely two, single-spaced pages. The paper's thin and brittle texture reflected impatience as well as haste, inattention as well as lack of development.

From the initial and most important discovery of the need to slow down certain consequences follow. One is a rectification of desire, to use Confucius's term as translated by Ezra Pound. What *Ta Hio*, or *The Great Digest*, records and teaches, is what the essay is all about: unobstructed penetration into the human heart and subsequent unblinkered revelation of what it treasures:

> The great learning ... takes root in clarifying the way wherein the intelligence increases through the process of looking straight into one's own heart and acting on the results; it is rooted in watching with affection the way people grow; it is rooted in coming to rest, being at ease in perfect equity.[19]

"Rooted." Could any other word better describe the essay: placed, settled, committed to cultivation? "Watching with affection the way people grow"—the essayist on his or her daily rounds, engaged in affirming life's newness and joy. "Looking straight into one's own heart"—the way Joan Didion exposes and probes our tendentious moralizing and the way E. B. White identifies honesty and candor as "the basic ingredient" in essaying. And finally, that rest and equity that is the essay's birthright, translated as the poise and balance that comes with judicious assaying, which Montaigne honored in Seneca, referring to him as *"ondoyant et divers."*[20]

Indeed, essayists never forget that composition lies at the root and the heart of life as of writing, that both partake of three inseparable notions of "composition": making, writing, and balancing. Montaigne hinted at it when he averred that "to compose our character" is our primary "duty," and Sam Pickering conserves the tradition in linking the composing of his life with the composing of (simple) sentences: "writing has taught me, and I have labored not so much to compose sentences as to compose my life.... [M]y days are composed, not of lurid prose and purple moments, but of calm of mind and forthright, workaday sentences."[21]

Taking up the essay—and setting aside the definite, confining, and exclusive article or treatise—reflects a reorientation, a conversion to a set of values distinctive in texture from all-too-familiar and now-aggrandized ones. Scott Sanders suggests this difference in his splendid account of the individual voice in "The Singular First Person." It is spelled out in Richard Selzer's equally splendid essay "A Worm from My Notebook" (incidentally, exemplary in the way it becomes unmistakably an essay by yoking reflection to what might otherwise be a *mere* short story). Here is Selzer, revealing the essay's kind of subject, its texture, and its process, rooted in patient and respectful observation and treatment of concrete, particular details:

> Were I a professor of the art of writing, I would coax my students to eschew all great and noble concepts—politics, women's liberation or any of the matters that affect society as a whole. There are no "great" subjects for the creative writer; there are only the singular details of a single human life. Just as there are no great subjects, there are no limits to the imagination. Send it off, I would urge my students, to wander into the side trails, the humblest burrows, to seek out the exceptional and the mysterious. . . . Fine writing can spring from the most surprising sources. Take parasitology, for instance. There is no more compelling drama than the life cycle of *Dracunculus medinensis*, the Guinea worm. Only to tell the story of its life and death is to peel away layers of obscurity, to shed light upon the earth and all of its creatures. That some fifty million of us are even now infested with this worm is of no literary interest whatsoever. Always, it is the affliction of one human being that captures the imagination. So it was with the passion of Jesus Christ; so it is with the infestation of single African man.

Then suddenly Selzer poses a question as the paragraph continues, and he proceeds to admit, quite understandably, that toward his created character, this single man the product of his imagination, he feels what can only be described as love:

> Shall we write the story together? A Romance of Parasitology? Let me tell you how it goes thus far. I will give you a peek into my notebook where you will see me struggling to set words down on a blank piece of paper. At first whimsically, capriciously, even insincerely. Later, in dead earnest. You will see at precisely what moment the writer ceases to think of his character as an instrument to be manipulated and think of him as someone with whom he has fallen in love. For it is always, must always be, a matter of love.[22]

So much matters and tells here: from that love the writer feels when his character becomes no longer an object but a person, to the clear implication that writing is genuine only when its creation is an *incarnation*. "Always," it bears repeating, "it is the affliction of one human being that captures the imagination." For whatever reason, this necessity poses arguably the greatest obstacle for beginning essay writers, weaned, as they long have been, on the quite erroneous notion that the form they are practicing, being nonfiction, is merely opinionative, perhaps argumentative, in any case an unimaginative statement or exploration directed by the demands of truth understood as unwavering and absolute commitment to verifiable facts peppered with speculations that, being cerebral, are also free of the creative taint. Typically, my students want to begin with a "great" subject, or at least a feasible facsimile of one, like Jayhawk-mania. By beginning at the wrong end, with the outcome—or, sometimes, the finish line—they neglect what alone bears literary interest: the experience of the singular human being. What the student writers need, in other words, is also what

Confucius wisely puts forth: to look straight into their hearts and see what they feel and how.

Selzer makes the point, too, that lies at the root of my asseverations against "gross and violent stimulants." The imagination is dulled by them, reduced to a state of torpor. Selzer urges us to send our imaginations off and let them wander—a line out for a walk. Wordsworth focuses too much, I cannot help but feel, on the effects on the mind, in the process narrowing and diverting attention to what you would suppose as his emphasis. "The mind" sounds too intellectual, too ratiocinative, and exclusive of other faculties and powers. Swift taught us, I should think, if nothing else, that man is not a rational animal but one *rationis capax*; without imagination, as Goya averred, man is just an animal.

The Romantics knew a lot about imagination, Wordsworth certainly prominently among them. They attribute great power to it, Wordsworth in *The Prelude*, his friend Coleridge in *Biographia Literaria*, Keats in brilliant remarks offered modestly in letters. Despite differences, they unite in differing from Cynthia Ozick's much later location of the source of morality; if for them it lies in the sympathetic imagination, for Ozick memory does the trick, the ancient Hebrews able "to envision the stranger's heart" *because* they had experienced slavery in Egypt. She makes a powerful although finally unconvincing case, pushing too hard (as she does in "The Riddle of the Ordinary," peremptory in her dismissal of Christian claims). No more sympathetic to Christianity and its "pious frauds" than Ozick, Keats got it right, I reckon, in describing the "poetical character," which he opposes to the "wordsworthian or egotistical sublime." Keats is important because, unlike Ozick, he recognizes the psychological context in which imagination executes its greatest work, specifically the moral force deriving from its address of egotism; but, second, and of nearly equal importance, Keats also, again unlike Ozick, links transcendence of egotism—what I call "getting out of self"—and writing, the latter being the result precisely of imagination's moral engagement with the former. Here is Keats, in an 1818 letter to his lawyer friend Richard Woodhouse:

> As to the poetical Character itself, (I mean that sort of which, if I am any thing, I am a Member; that sort distinguished from the wordsworthian or egotistical sublime; which is a thing per se and stands alone) it is not itself—it has no self—it is every thing and nothing—It has no character—it enjoys light and shade; it lives in gusto, be it foul or fair, high or low, rich or poor, mean or elevated—It has as much delight in conceiving an Iago as an Imogen. What shocks the virtuous philosop[h]er, delights the camelion Poet. . . . A Poet is the most unpoetical of any thing in existence; because he has no Identity—he is continually in for—and filling some other Body—The Sun, the Moon, the Sea and Men and Women. . . . the poet has none; no identity. . . .[23]

By projecting oneself into other creatures and things, by informing them, the poet, says Keats, is the opposite of "an Egotist," whom he earlier described as one—again, his example is Wordsworth—who "brood[s] and peacock[s]" over his "speculations": in that letter to John Hamilton Reynolds, Keats asserts, "We hate poetry that has a palpable design upon us—and if we do not agree, seems to put its hand in its breeches pocket. Poetry should be great & unobtrusive, a thing which enters into one's soul, and does not startle it or amaze it with itself but with its subject."[24] It is just that "Impersonal theory" that T. S. Eliot made the Modernists' war cry in another revolution of sensibility, this one overturning Wordsworth. Although E. B. White calls himself and his fellow essayists self-centered and egoistical, the form of which he was a master actually joins forces with Keats and Eliot, for the essayist's job consists in dramatizing—and *incarnating*—how it feels to hold such-and-such a position.

In a famous passage in the essay "On Experience," the last of his *Essais*, Montaigne declared that "To compose our character is our duty, not to compose books, and to win, not battles and provinces, but order and tranquillity in our conduct. Our great and glorious masterpiece," he concluded, "is to live appropriately."[25] The infinitive with which Montaigne begins points in two different but related directions, both made clear via his zeugma: the "father" of "the fourth genre" is talking about composition as both the art of writing and the writing or achieving of "order and tranquillity in our conduct"—and suggesting the way the former may function in the creation and achievement of the latter.

The connection that Montaigne made between writing well ("nature's chief masterpiece," said Pope in *An Essay on Criticism*, quoting the Duke of Buckingham) and living well has been duly noted, elaborated, and promoted by anthologist Lydia Fakundiny and perpetuated by, among others, Sam Pickering, who, in "Composing a Life," explores the link between a way of life and the kinds of sentences one writes. While making sentences neither so simple and declarative as Pickering advises, nor so "comely and muscular" as Cynthia Ozick praises (and makes), I want to second Montaigne's notion. Except implicitly and suggestively, I shall not argue for the connection between living appropriately and writing well. I shall instead (and only!) contend that at the heart of both senses of composition—writing and achieving "order and tranquillity" in our lives—is that simplicity that Pickering proclaims and that Thoreau preached so dramatically. I mean the nevertheless difficult requirement of slowing down, which not even E. B. White (nor his Cornell teacher Will Strunk, coauthor of the "little book" *Elements of Style*) quite managed to identify, isolate, and put in other words.

As Roland Barthes has pointed out, "for a long time writing was attended by great ceremony. In ancient Chinese society," to take a prominent example, "one prepared oneself for writing, for handling the ink brush, through an almost religious asceticism. In certain Christian monasteries of the Middle Ages, the copyists began their work only after a day of meditation." Barthes then admits that, to a degree, he practices some such ceremony, for instance switching from one pen to another, trying out new ones.[26] He also discusses other aspects of his own writing ritual, repeating his recognition of a certain entailed obsessiveness. He is by no means alone in requiring set procedures, the novelist-essayist-biographer Edmund White, for instance, being able to compose only in "very beautiful notebooks and with very beautiful pens."[27]

In an essay published in *JAC* and titled "On Writing Well: Or, Springing the Genie from the Inkpot," I also offered an apologia for writing, like Edmund White and Barthes and Hilaire Belloc, with "an easy pen."[28] I believe strongly, as I said there, that you write better when you compose with an instrument that you respect, that demands your best, that slows you down, and that you honor by putting forth your strongest and clearest effort. I claimed, too, as I still would, that the pen and the familiar essay make powerful and effective partners, sharing values, goals, perspectives, and character.

Slowing down is, after all, what the essay teaches and what success in the form requires.

"Taking a line out for a walk"—let's look again at Paul Klee's notion. If "the pen thinks for you," as Belloc claimed, it is perhaps because the writing controls, dictates, and determines the pen's movements. Authority, although not responsibility, shifts. If all this sounds too mystical, think of Barthes, the arch-structuralist and semiotician, who endorsed the overthrow of "that old myth which continues to present language as the instrument of thought, inwardness, passion, or whatever, and consequently presents writing as a simple instrumental process." Rejecting the "Bic style," he thus opposed writing that is merely "churning out copy, writing that merely transcribes thought."[29] Barthes elaborates this same point in his book on Japan, *Empire of Signs*, distinguishing the writing there from that in both Europe and the United States, where it is too often merely instrumental rather than productive, that is, creative.

In Zen terms, the act of writing that I describe, predicated on deliberateness, patience, and respect, resembles the desired state of mindfulness, with the mind present to itself in a situation of extreme alertness and attention, so absorbed in the act it witnesses and is a party to that it virtually forgets about itself. This is akin to what Keats describes as "the poetical Character," distinguishing it from the "wordsworthian or egotistical sublime." The point, Keats declares, is that the true or genuine poet "has no Identity—he is continually in for—and filling some other Body." I understand Keats as proposing a kind of ec-stasy, with the poet capable of stepping outside himself and into "some other Body." In this situation, the mind is given over entirely to something else, what Belloc evidently means (while inverting the notion of mindfulness) when he advocates, as in prayer, such activity as you perform, "as it were, with half your mind: that happier half, the half that does not bother."[30] The voracious and rapacious ego, ever meddling, always assertive and willful and interfering in the reception of otherness, is thus eclipsed, or transcended.

Still, to write well, the mind must be fully present. And not just present, for not just any mind can make essays. In addition to keen observation and scrupulous attention to detail (in both the gathering and the representing), the mind of the writer needs be open, receptive, and willing to brook something outside and beyond the familiar, the expected, the quick and efficient. A certain confidence must exist, to be sure, as well as poise and composure—the mind must, in other words, be in a state of composure in order to compose. Or is it, rather, that composing creates composure and poise? Here too it's difficult to distinguish and say that we can pinpoint the exact moment or the exact difference: whether composure pre-exists the writing or emerges in, through, and by means of it.

It helps, in any case, if that mind has a stock of ideas and references and ready access to them, a knowledge, in other words, of books and life, in both of which it is well versed and that it is thus able to draw upon. These references should lie just at hand, ready to enlist as a situation is explored, an idea or feeling is probed. What happens in the act of composing is that the mind, slowing down, loses some of its assertive power, primacy beginning to shift toward both the subconscious and the subject of the writing. In the event, the mind does not experience this shift or feel loss, which loss the failure to acknowledge confirms. In a state of poise, balance, and composure, the mind feels neither anxious nor frenetic: at rest, it lies low while something else happens. The richer the texture of the now-existing mind, the more rises to the surface to greet and mingle with the direction/will of the writing.

At this juncture, the essay begins to work against the considerable pull toward straight narrative and "pure" autobiography alike. Slowing down leads to reflection, but also, with the mind composed, the essay, in its very reflections, moves toward poetry. I refer not to its obviously lyrical nature but, rather, to poetry's fundamental nature, which I understand (in Pound's words) as "language charged with meaning to the utmost possible degree."[31] No one writes poetry quickly or efficiently, and the essay begins to share the realm of poetry, if ever so lightly, when the writer, poised and composed and so open to the direction of the writing, slows down sufficiently for "weight" to accumulate. An essay thus becomes charged with meaning—what was lacking in my student's paper on her school's illustrious basketball tradition. All of us have experiences, certainly enough to fuel our writing, but, as another student once put it, few of us are able to find—to mine and then assay—the meaning of them. The reason why is often blindingly simple: in haste, we do not take the time.

Relying on revision to sort through and find for my atomistic building blocks an identifiable and coherent structure, I had for too long been unable—or unwilling—to take a line out for a walk. I could not, would not, sustain thought, which I vainly sought to contain and capture, mistaken in believing that if instead I released it, it would soon escape or vanish. I could not let go, still grasping, still enchained to the willful ego, despite my conversion from the article to the essay.

It is different now since I gave up alcohol and took up the fountain pen. Since I have chronicled elsewhere both climactic events, I shall repeat here only that, even if the latter pales in comparison to the former, still my conversion to "an easy pen" bears an importance that no doubt eludes reason. At any rate, I now look forward to taking up my pen in the morning, no longer anxious before the blank page, no longer needing some substance to jump-start my essay.

I delight in the feel of the pen and, equally, in feeling at one with the instrument as we glide, slide together across the page, and I rejoice, again equally, in the process. In this material process, which I distinguish from the central *acts* of writing and of creating, rather more ethereal and spiritual endeavors, I am already as a dancer becoming indistinguishable from the dance. This process, I dare to say, has the feel for me now of a religious ceremony. It's as if, sitting down at my cluttered desk, coffee in hand and pen across the legal pad at the mark where I stopped before, I enter a nearly sacred place that, itself, has the power to make me ready to receive blessing.

Here, sin is known as outside interference, whether Rebecca's good-morning kiss, the insentient jangling of the telephone, or the irruptive memory of a mundane task awaiting. Alone with pen and paper, morning or afternoon, when I compose I am as close perhaps as I shall ever be to sacred time, because for a while nothing else can matter. If drink was once my golden calf, a false idol, the pen is now my medium, the connection between the Muse and me. Or is it that I have become the medium, in the process no longer myself but the instrument of that which writes through me? Not knowing, I count on such "negative capability" as Keats equated with the acceptance of half-knowledge.

I do not pretend to some *ek-stasis*, but I shall claim an inching—rather than an itching—toward transcendence; but if it be that, or something like it, it is clearly material and clearly rooted in the here and now: transcendence in and by means of the immanent, for this is reality felt with great keenness. Never before has my mind felt so clear as when I take a line out for a walk; nor have I felt freer than when submitting to the line, the line of thinking, feeling, and reflecting, and the line of words my "easy pen" makes, caressing the page.

Whatever else it may be, the process of writing bears the mark of ceremony, with its due observances. These conspire to promote that freedom from the ego's demands that I have sought to describe: separation—if not retreat—from outside attractions and responsibilities. For a while, writing puts me in a situation best described as monastic, when I am free of the ways and worries of the world to concentrate on the truly important. In her magnificent essay on writing titled "The Seam of the Snail" (formerly, "Excellence") Cynthia Ozick confesses that "The sentence I am writing now is my cabin and my shell, compact, self-sufficient." In fact, she writes,

> . . . nothing matters to me so much as a comely and muscular sentence. It is my narrow strait, this snail's road; the track of the sentence I am writing now; and when I have eked out the wet substance, ink or blood, that is its mark, I will begin the next sentence. Only in treading out sentences am I perfectionist; but then there is nothing else I know how to do, or take much interest in.[32]

As long as I am engaged in the ceremony commonly called writing, I feel as Ozick does; outside that ceremony, all is different, and whether or not she would grant it, I reckon that the difference makes all the difference.

PARADOX ABOUNDING
TENSION AND THE VIA MEDIA NATURE OF THE ESSAY

―

Man's base nature is the outcome of self-assertion.
Daisetz T. Suzuki, *Zen and Japanese Culture*

Then I dare; I will also essay to be.
Ralph Waldo Emerson, *Journal*

Essays, however, hang somewhere on a line between two sturdy poles:
this is what I think, and this is what I am.
Edward Hoagland, "What I Think, What I Am"

―

THE GREATEST INTERNAL THREAT to the West may be the culture of self-esteem, a much-ballyhooed legacy of the Renaissance and the Reformation and an essential component of the unleashed individualism that the French Revolution, Romanticism, and modernism developed in fearful but not unforeseen ways. Postmodernism has challenged "the autonomy of the individual," as did, from a rather different perception, Modernist (not to be confused with modern) writers nearly a century ago. The common enemy is the same individualism and belief in the sanctity of the private self that Wordsworth declared and celebrated as revolutionary in the Preface to *Lyrical Ballads* and incarnated in his great work *The Prelude* (subtitled *Growth of a Poet's Mind: An Autobiographical Poem*). These ideas stem from the religious enthusiasm and dissent that fueled the Reformation, they took on new life preceding and during the English civil war, and they burned in the memory and imagination of neo-Augustan writers, for whom regicide and the re-establishment of a commonwealth or some form of theocracy remained an ever-present danger. Individualism, though, like kudzu, is swarming, voracious, and hardy. There is no undoing what "the priesthood of all believers" wrought. There are, however, better and worse ways of dealing with what may have begun as an undeniable "Good."

In the present climate and with so much sustenance and support, the cult of self-esteem flourishes as a byproduct of regnant individualism. Television hourly promotes and celebrates it, and modern education appears as little more than the formalization of the mindless patterings often available from Oprah, Doctor Phil, and Richard Simmons. The facilitation of self-esteem long ago threatened teaching, and learning diminished even before Foucault equated discipline and punishment. Who now subscribes to or even appears willing to listen to calls such as Eliot's for "prayer, observance, discipline, thought and action" (*The Dry Salvages, Four Quartets*)?[1] Who now even entertains—the word is depressingly precise—the possibility that *my* opinion is not as good as *anyone* else's, that being true to oneself may be dangerous rather than salutary, that independence, self-sufficiency, and assertiveness prove often to be forms of indulgence and sophomoric defiance and rebelliousness that should be discouraged and restrained rather than cultivated and promoted? Rousseau has never before enjoyed so much influence, even if unacknowledged. I must, in other words, feel good about myself, noble though savage, to the point of brooking no challenge to my "self-worth." All the while, the puny, pusillanimous self grows fat and lazy—and all the more willful and determined, enjoying privilege and place never before accorded it in the East or the West. To put it in terms familiar to Dryden, Swift, and Pope, ours is a "*latitudinarian*" age, ours an "*easie God*" that "instructs Thee to *rebell*"; thus writes a severe critic of "the private spirit" and "fanaticism" in his remarkably prescient layman's faith: "*Thou* art *Justice* in the *last Appeal*" (*Religio Laici* 96, 95).[2]

Recently in my advanced composition class, a graduating English major said that what he had learned over four years was little more than how to respond to questions: "All you have to do is begin, 'In my opinion. . . .'" Exaggeration and melodramatic effect aside, there is woeful truth here, for judgment and comparative evaluation, based in knowledge, thoughtful consideration, and a rational and defensible sense of standards, have next to no place in the prevailing conception of literary studies, which were once historical and objective and now are theoretical, subjective, and political. I see little evidence of a desire to distinguish between excellence and mediocrity. No wonder that students leave the university supposing their opinion is equal to Pope's, Eliot's, Dante's, or Homer's. Leveling exacts a heavy toll.

It is bad enough that we insist on "leveling the playing-field," democratizing "opinion," and in the end embellishing the image we carry of our self. "Don't make me feel bad about myself" is the requirement made of faculties and increasingly enforced by administrators, who aim to please the consumer and keep him paying the exorbitant bills. No matter how partial, ill-informed, or misguided, my "opinion" thus goes unchallenged. To be sure, I may be taught to read against the grain of authors' apparent intentions, to probe advertising for its not-so-subtle manipulations, even to acknowledge that *I* harbor residual sexism, classism, and racism. But am I ever asked to enter that horrific "heart of darkness" that is not merely a civilization's or an author's, but *my own*? The one thing I surely can fix, that which I should rectify before setting about to change others or the world, is me. But our culture of self-esteem militates, despite its self-centeredness, against the kind of inner examination that can lead to correction. Were I to look honestly into my heart, I might think less well of myself, which, in our me-culture, would be the worst of sinning.

IN THIS LEADEN AGE, besotted on self, no literary form has been more widely or warmly embraced—nearly to the point of lionization—than nonfiction parading the author's private life. As the memoir has far outstripped biography in popularity, thoughts, feelings, and desires have swum to the foreground, along with confessions, exposures, recriminations, rationalizations, doubts—and much hand-wringing. Where autobiography was once the province of the famous and the rich—it was their actions, their public lives that compelled readers—now offering slices of life is the province of Everyman, no matter how small his or her public contribution, so democratic has become the publication of the individual talent.

Ours is "the age of the memoir," proclaimed the *New York Times* not long ago, soon after, in fact, the announcement elsewhere that ours is "the age of the essay." Once thought to be dead with mindless good riddance, the essay has been enjoying a remarkable renaissance, fed by the same source of desire for nonfiction and self-revelation as the memoir and some TV talk shows. So closely related are the two forms that they are sometimes indistinguishable. Not surprisingly, the personal essay is now the form of choice, the familiar essay providing little competition. The standard anthology is *The Art of the Personal Essay*, edited by Phillip Lopate, and it is more influential than Lydia Fakundiny's earlier and quite sensible *The Art of the Essay*.

We customarily extol the essay for its individuality and its uniqueness of perspective, its particular and distinctive "take" on things. Accordingly, we celebrate the essay's voice, rich, attentive, wise-sounding, sometimes cranky and cantankerous, not always lovable but interesting, typically opinionated and feisty. It "conveys," says Edward Hoagland, "the quality of the author's mind."[3] If you don't like or trust the voice you hear speaking to you, if it grates or fails to charm, if it offers no distinctive slant or possesses no singularity, you will, avers Annie Dillard, very likely stop reading. *Her* voice is immediately recognizable, as are, I dare say, those of Sam Pickering, Cynthia Ozick, Richard Selzer, Dr. Johnson,

Bacon, and Montaigne. Social and cultural distinctions being blurred, if not sacrificed and even erased, we crave difference and so look to and find in the essay some old-fashioned reassurances.

The individualistic nature of the essay and its congenital closeness to the memoir has recently been described by Scott Russell Sanders. A successful practitioner of the form himself, Sanders makes clear the reasons for its current revival and modern culture's need of it:

> In this era of prepackaged thought, the essay is the closest thing we have, on paper, to a record of the individual mind at work and play. It is an amateur's raid in a world of specialists. Feeling overwhelmed by data, random information, the flotsam and jetsam of mass culture, we relish the spectacle of a single consciousness making sense of a portion of the chaos.[4]

"What I Think, What I Am" Edward Hoagland titled his pithy peregrination around the essay's individualistic virtues, tying its particular kind of reflection to epistemology. E. B. White, earlier, was less tactful, despite apparent irony, acknowledging the form's inherent egoism and not merely its individualistic nature. White well describes the work of the personal essayist, following Montaigne's lead. The essay thus feeds into, and derives sustenance from, the culture of self-esteem—the me-culture—I have lamented. At the same time, the essay's inwardness, the inner direction of its will, suggests the possibility of that self-scrutiny lacking today.

Montaigne's essays pursued a slippery slope; rather than examine the self's limitations—and its rapacious nature, its heart of darkness—he opted in his self-consciousness instead to map his self's topography. Like Thoreau, who opens *Walden* by saying, "I should not talk so much about myself if there were anybody else whom I knew as well," Montaigne is a surveyor, taking the measure of the territory that is the self, engaging in "*home*-cosmography."[5]

Historically, of course, such mapping, which appears objective, has led to deep probing of the self, its crevasses and its mazy ways. Recent essayists, especially, are the most personal, confessional, and even indulgent; some readers find that their explorations amount sometimes to "navel-gazing." All along, though, essayists have resembled Hamlet, if not "sicklied o'er with the pale cast of thought," at the very least introspective and self-conscious. He, of course, dared whether to be or not to be; Emerson later, bolder, self-reliant, and assured, declared, "Then I dare: I will also essay to be."[6] He thus has inspired more than one commentator to link essaying with being. In fact, Phillip Lopate comes perilously close to making the essay what it never has been: philosophy. Introducing *The Art of the Personal Essay* and aware that he may be making "excessive claims," he declares:

> In the final analysis, the personal essay represents a mode of being. It points a way for the self to function with relative freedom in an uncertain world. Skeptical yet gyroscopically poised, undeceived but finally tolerant of flaws and inconsistencies, this mode of being suits the modern existential situation, which Montaigne first diagnosed. His recognition that human beings were surrounded by darkness, with nothing particularly solid to cling to, led to a philosophical acceptance that one had to make oneself up from moment to moment.[7]

It is by no means necessary to accept such a representation of "the human condition"—indeed, I have earlier limited "darkness" to the situation *made* by man that results in a "modern existential situation" only for those who spin private interpretations out of their beclouded soul.

Eliot, for one, found Montaigne "insidious," respecting but ultimately rejecting his way of thinking:

> ... of all authors Montaigne is one of the least destructible. You could as well dissipate a fog by flinging hand-grenades into it. For Montaigne is a fog, a gas, a fluid, insidious element. He does not reason, he insinuates, charms, and influences; or if he reasons, you must be prepared for his having some other design upon you than to convince you by his argument.[8]

Distinguishing Montaigne from Pascal, whose *Pensées* he is introducing and whose path toward "acceptance" of "rejection and elimination" he endorses, Eliot proceeds to apposite remarks on doubt and inwardness:

> The picture of Montaigne which offers itself first to our eyes, that of the original and independent solitary personality, absorbed in amused analysis of himself, is deceptive. Montaigne's is no *limited* Pyrrhonism, like that of Voltaire, Renan, or France. He exists, so to speak, on a plan[e] of numerous concentric circles, the most apparent of which is the small inmost circle, a personal puckish scepticism which can be easily aped if not imitated. But what makes Montaigne a very great figure is that he succeeded, God knows how—for Montaigne very likely did not know that he had done it—it is not the sort of thing that men *can* observe about themselves, for it is essentially bigger than the individual's consciousness—he succeeded in giving expression to the scepticism of *every*

human being. For every man who thinks and lives by thought must have his own scepticism, that which stops at the question, that which ends in denial, or that which leads to faith and which is somehow integrated into the faith which transcends it. And Pascal, as the type of one kind of religious believer, which is highly passionate and ardent, but passionate only through a powerful and regulated intellect, is in the first sections of his unfinished Apology for Christianity facing unflinchingly the demon of doubt which is inseparable from the spirit of belief.[9]

Eliot thus acknowledges the necessity of doubt, thereby deconstructing the opposition to belief while forcefully criticizing Montaigne for stopping short: that is, according to the defender of Pascal, the "wily old Gascon" failed to proceed in, through, and by means of nearly congenital doubt. The pattern of thinking that Eliot puts forth here is important and exemplary, as we shall see.

For the moment my purpose is more limited. To help draw the necessary distinction between Montaigne's mapping of his self and an alternative that has never been fully realized in the essay—and that perhaps never can be—I turn to his great admirer Alexander Pope. Juxtapose, if you will, Montaigne's characteristic skeptical question *"que sais-je?"* with the well-known opening verses of *An Essay on Man*—like the earlier *An Essay on Criticism*, a true essay, although in verse—that embody the traditional Socratic injunction:

> Know then thyself, presume not God to scan;
> The proper study of Mankind is Man.
> Plac'd on this isthmus of a middle state,

> A being darkly wise, and rudely great:
> With too much knowledge for the Sceptic side,
> With too much weakness for the Stoic's pride,
> He hangs between; in doubt to act, or rest,
> In doubt to deem himself a God, or Beast;
> In doubt his Mind or Body to prefer,
> Born but to die, and reas'ning but to err;
> Alike in ignorance, his reason such,
> Whether he thinks too little, or too much:
> Chaos of Thought and Passion, all confus'd;
> Still by himself abus'd, or disabus'd;
> Created half to rise, and half to fall;
> Great lord of all things, yet a prey to all;
> Sole judge of Truth, in endless Error hurl'd:
> The glory, jest, and riddle of the world! (2.1–18)[10]

The contrast and balance of the lines here embody and incarnate the message: man is an in-between creature, neither completely one thing nor absolutely another. Recognizing this, Pope cannot be either a Skeptic or a Stoic, although he may sometimes be one and at another time the other. In a sense, this position itself smacks of skepticism, not of "*limited*" Pyrrhonism but more pervasive. But in any case, it smacks little of Montaigne. For one thing, Pope does not put forth a question—*que sais-je?*—but, rather, provides an answer. Nor is the poet speaking of the "I," but instead delivering a message, using the imperative. That injunction, moreover, bears little of the psychological texture of Montaigne's "home-cosmography." Its end is certainly moral. If Montaigne essays to know himself for the sake of knowing, Pope—in Baconian fashion—exhorts us to know ourselves in order to correct and improve ourselves. Improvement might result for the Frenchman, but it would be a by-product. What he says in an essay about a near-death experience reveals his distance from Pope. The instruction Montaigne derived from a serious fall from his horse and the ensuing trauma may have been preparation for death, but only in the limited and morally neutral sense of becoming familiar with its near-relation, not at all with settling accounts, making amends, or becoming penitent: Montaigne thus severely limits the idea of preparing for death.

In urging *men* to know their limitations and their proclivity to folly and vice, Pope is both near to and far from the kind of "looking straight into the heart" that Pound shares with Eliot and other Christians. Pope, in fact, does not engage in inner or private examination, although he everywhere insists on the necessity of judgment and correction. Contemplation rarely makes for strong writing (although it may lead to it)—Izaak Walton's *Compleat Angler* is a notable exception. Yet the potential resides in the essay, theoretically if not structurally, for the representation of penitence and humility, the fundamentals of the Christian life, as Eliot has affirmed.

As to the directional force of the essay, no one has surpassed Sanders in the afore-cited "The Singular First Person." He accepts without question or hesitation the form's defining individualism: what the poets, in Eliot's famous formulation, must "surrender," the essayist must cultivate and preserve. However, a potentially troublesome note emerges, although Sanders seems unaware of it:

> The essay is a haven for the private, idiosyncratic voice in an era of anonymous babble. Like the bland-burgers served in their millions

along our highways, most language served up in public these days is textureless, tasteless mush. On television, over the phone, in the newspaper, wherever humans bandy words about, we encounter more and more abstractions, more empty formulas. Think of the pablum ladled out by politicians. Think of the fluffy white bread of advertising. Think, lord help us, of committee reports.

Turning to the corruption of language, Sanders strikes a note less like Romantic individualists and more like the Modernists Pound, Eliot, and Joyce. From a vilification of abstraction, Sanders turns to an endorsement of the inductive, or *a posteriori*, nature of essaying, a Baconian note that rests in tension alongside his predominant "personal" and individualist valuations: "By contrast, the essay remains stubbornly concrete and particular: it confronts you with an oil-smeared toilet at the Sunoco station, a red vinyl purse shaped like a valentine heart, a bow-legged dentist hunting deer with an elephant gun." Sanders concludes by linking language and politics, á la Orwell—no Royalists here, although Orwell, of course, managed an Arnoldian open-mindedness regarding the socialism he generally espoused:

As Orwell forcefully argued, and as dictators seem to agree, such a bypassing of abstractions, such an insistence on the concrete, is a politically subversive act. Clinging to this door, that child, this grief, following the zigzag notions of an inquisitive mind, the essay renews language and clears trash from the springs of thought. A century and a half ago, in the rousing manifesto entitled *Nature*, Emerson called on a new generation of writers to cast off the hand-me-down rhetoric of the day, to "pierce this rotten diction and fasten words again to visible things." The essayist aspires to do just that.[11]

The essayist does, indeed, direct his attention, mind, and soul to the immediate, the concrete, and the particular—the implied locus of value for all who pursue this protean form. In so doing, the essayist implies criticism and certainly expresses wariness of systems, which he usually rejects outright. Reasoning "upward" from what he knows, rather than "downward" from some theory or imagined truth, the essayist witnesses to the supreme value of experience. But the particulars experienced, tried, and tested—both essayed and assayed—do not require a uniqueness in the perceiver.

Inherent in the essay, I am suggesting, practically from its inception, is a countervailing tendency to what E. B. White identified as its "congenital self-centeredness." Those characteristics linking it to the Reformation and, later, Dissent coexist with an equally definitive *a posteriorism*, a concomitant of the empirical habit attributable to the first English essayist, Francis Bacon, scientist and author of learned treatises as well as of *The Essayes or Counsels, Civil and Morall*, a first version of which appeared in 1597, only a few years after Montaigne's seemingly more modest *Essais*. A man of greater knowledge and wider experience than Montaigne, Bacon explores not himself but familiar topics, offering ready advice and steady counsel. In writings he thought original (despite Seneca and Plutarch, whom he knew, and Oriental essayists such as Sei Shonagon and Kenko, whom he could not), Montaigne boldly asserts his intentions and his prerogatives, proclaiming his right to write *about* himself, *for* himself. Bacon, on the other hand, teaches, prescribing and proscribing (cf. "Of Studies," "Of Boldness"). Montaigne does sometimes feel the tug outward that Bacon explored, as do familiar essayists like Woolf and White, Johnson and Didion, and Arnold and Eliot. He says at one point, signaling both his fundamental orientation and a perhaps ineradicable tension, "And yet it should not be held against me if I publish what I write. What is useful to me may also *by accident* be useful to another" (my italics).[12] Bacon and those who follow his path leave no instruction to "accident."

The problem I am unfolding Eliot confronts as "tradition and the individual talent," the title of an important essay included in his 1920 volume *The Sacred Wood*. As revolutionary as Wordsworth's Preface, against which it stands as anti-Romantic and Modernist, Eliot's essay calls for an "Impersonal theory of poetry" and the urgent necessity of the poet to "surrender" his personality to something outside himself. Eliot by no means intended to sanction aridity or sterility; as the novelist Jeanette Winterson has recently put it, "Eliot is an emotional poet and the poets he particularly loved, the Metaphysicals and Dante, are poets of feeling but tightly kept." And indeed, feeling, not intellect, is the poetic basis for this very intellectual poet. His notion of poetry "demands a concentration *away* from Self, an impersonality that allows other realities to find a voice that is more than reported speech"; "the space that art creates," moreover, continues Winterson, "is space outside of a relentless self, a meditation that gives both release and energy."[13] Eliot devoted his career—as poet, essayist, and dramatist—to the war against self, personality in poetry, and individualism. The institutionalizing of these efforts is represented by his famous embrace in 1927 of Anglo-Catholicism, classicism, and Royalism. And yet Eliot renders quite complex the relation of the individual to that power outside itself, eschewing a simple either/or choice. He in fact echoes his friend Pound in seeking to "make it new," an effort incarnate in his poetry, for Eliot recognized that mere conformity to the past is hardly the answer; it results in slavish imitation, stale and powerless. "In a peculiar sense," Eliot states clearly, the poet will be aware that

> he must inevitably be judged by the standards of the past. I say judged, not amputated, by them; not judged to be as good as, or worse or better than, the dead; and certainly not judged by the canons of dead critics. It is a judgment, a comparison, in which two things are measured by each other. To conform merely would be for the new work not really to conform at all; it would not be new, and would therefore not be a work of art. And we do not quite say that the new is more valuable because it fits in; but its fitting in is a test of its value—a test, it is true, which can only be slowly and cautiously applied, for we are none of us infallible judges of conformity. We say: it appears to conform, and is perhaps individual, or it appears individual, and may conform; but we are hardly likely to find that it is one and not the other.[14]

As Eliot surrenders his personality, making a work that is other than self-expressive and transcendent of narrowly autobiographical interests, so he writes "not merely with his own generation in his bones, but with a feeling that the whole of the literature of Europe from Homer and within it the whole of the literature of his own country has a simultaneous existence and composes a simultaneous order." Eliot scrupulously points out that "the existing order," or tradition, "is complete before the new work arrives; for order to persist after the supervention of novelty, the *whole* existing order must be, if ever so slightly, altered; and so the relations, proportions, values of each work of art toward the whole are readjusted," and this, he concludes, "is conformity between the old and the new." It is not, then, "preposterous that the poet should be altered by the present as the present is directed by the past."¹⁵

In the final analysis, Eliot's representation of the complex relation between the individual and tradition recalls, indeed echoes, Dryden's take in *Religio Laici* on the layman's relation to tradition. Echoes should hardly be surprising, given Eliot's knowledge of and respect and admiration for the neo-Augustan poet (in 1924, he published *Homage to John Dryden*, followed by an edition of Dryden's *Of Dramatick Poesie* in 1928, and four years later *John Dryden: The Poet, the Dramatist, the Critic*—not incidentally, the three "phases" of his own writing career). Dryden would have the layman "surrender" too, evincing an Eliotesque opposition to the "thoroughgoing": since *complete* submission to tradition would land the layman in the clutches of the (Catholic) Church, Dryden insists on consultation and then outward acceptance, if disagreements remain. Eliot too rejects a monolithic and irrefragable sense of tradition, believing it alterable by the individual's contributions as he must know and respect and write from within it. What matters even more, I think, is that Dryden and Eliot posit a common enemy: the unreined individual, listening to and acting on "the private spirit" with little or no respect for authority outside his own rapacious self.

IN ELIOT'S FORMULATION, as in Dryden's (though somewhat differently), tension exists and persists between the individual and tradition. Tension exists in any relationship, of course, although it is not always constitutive. For years I recognized some such tension as characteristic of the essay, at least part of which Scott Sanders evidently intuited in bringing together the form's quest for singularity of voice with its equally forceful embrace of the experiential, the empirical, and the inductive. I am tempted to call these distinctions the Montaignian and the Baconian kinds, perhaps less important as forms of the essay than as characterizing the different, even competing directions within it. I had, as I say, some inchoate notion of such constitutive tension years ago; indeed, in an essay titled "In Other Words: Gardening for Love— The Work of the Essayist" and first published in *The Kenyon Review*, I wrote of a peculiarly "in-between" nature, a sort of *via media*. If the essay, I then said, seems pieced and patched together like a quilt, it also seems natural—in several important ways. It appears at once as a natural growth and as a constructed thing. It is, in more than one respect, a threshold being, an "in-between" thing, hanging indeterminately—but not unhappily—between knowledge and art, creation and cognition, thought and things, writing and living, nature and cultivation, involving a little of both and all.[16]

We can better appreciate the *via media* nature of the essay if we reflect, as is little done, on its deep connection to religious Dissent and Northern "enthusiasm." The contemporary Irish writer and poet Tom Paulin opens the path to understanding in introducing his collection of essays *Writing to the Moment*. Flooded by the great Romantic essayist William Hazlitt, to whom he subsequently devoted a monograph, Paulin describes "this eager, volatile, intense form of consciousness" that he admires as "one of the legacies of the Reformation." "The free individual conscience and the accompanying concept of free speech," writes Paulin, "shape the critical essay—in Hazlitt's phrase, proper expressions rise to the surface from the heat of the essayist's mind 'like bubbles on an agitated stream.'"[17] The zeal with which Hazlitt speaks—sermonizes, sometimes—cannot but remind readers of that "tradition" Swift excoriated in his unsparing treatment of Brother Jack and other "enthusiasts" in *A Tale of a Tub*: fancy indeed gets astride reason, producing a sort of madness. Paulin observes that the style of the famous (and notorious) *Edinburgh Review*, edited by Francis Jeffrey, had its origin around 1796 in a series of essays written by the Unitarian scholar William Taylor, and as a result, "Anyone who examines dissenting culture is bound to notice how many magazines and journals it produced."[18]

Geoffrey H. Hartman has similarly pointed to a certain zeal or enthusiasm in the essay and argued that it "is not separable from . . . religion." His focus too is the critical essay, itself never completely separable from the personal or the familiar. Hartman sides, in fact, with a "creative" sort of reading, one that attends closely to what he calls "the inner voice." In the manner of Dryden's "Fanaticks" and Swift's willful Brothers, we are actually being taught "not only to read the lines but also to hear the words, the words in the words, and the images of voice they suggest." This is, at once, Puritan, Romantic, and Gnostic (as well as Hebraic), and Hartman's "creative criticism" has appeared to many readers as the sort of willful distortion of "plain sense" that Swift roundly satirized. In Hartman's words, which apply to his own critical commentary (say, on Wordsworth, or on Derrida's *Glas*) about the work he extols (say, *Sartor Resartus* or Harold Bloom's avowedly revisionist and Gnostic readings), "An enthusiastic type of criticism replaces an English type which was, and continues to be despite Carlyle, a critique of enthusiasm." In the three chapters of *Criticism in the Wilderness* titled "The Sacred Jungle," themselves a counter-argument to Eliot's *The Sacred Wood*, Hartman offers these apposite remarks on the essay and the *via media*:

The relation of enthusiasm to political fanaticism is a fearful reality that hovers over English history and the establishment of *via media* institutions from the reign of Elizabeth on. Literary criticism like everything else became a *via media* institution. Though the fear of enthusiasm gradually receded into the *angustiae* of the Gothic novel it was given a temporary renewal by the French Revolution with its regicide, its Reign of Terror, and its atheistic religion of reason.[19]

AN "IN-BETWEEN" THING, the essay lives in tension, pulled both formally and historically in contrary directions: paradox abounding. At one and the same time, it appears artless and artful: a processual thing that knows its destination only in the arrival, although, in fact, that appearance of near-insouciance, wandering, and directionlessness is part of the charm, part of the rhetoric, part of the art subtly crafted by a writer skilled in the Polonian awareness that you best find direction by indirection. In any case, art coexists with the personal, without becoming awash in it: Woolfian control with self-expressiveness. According to Walter Pater, the essay subsists by means of its unmethodical method. Moreover, as Georg Lukács noted, whereas the essay seems to be about only the inconsequential and nonessential, and indeed merely the surface of these, it actually reaches for nothing less than "the Ultimate." The title Montaigne gave to the peregrinations of his mind—*Essais*—thus reveals, says Lukács, an "arrogant courtesy."[20]

You may need "the essayistic spirit" in order to write essays, which effort itself, however, appears responsible for creating that capaciousness. Truth certainly clings to Montaigne's reiterated notion that, in Lydia Fakundiny's words, "The doing, the writing itself, is both a path *to* knowing and a path *of* knowing." As I write, he declared, "I am 'forming my life.'"[21] So, then, essaying to be, do I "fashion" a self in the act of writing, as some believe, or must I already be an essayist, equipped with the wisdom and rectitude of that "spirit," in order to write in this demanding and rewarding form? Put differently, is the speaker who matters crucially to the success of the essay a required persona or the creation of the writing process?

Another point: the essay belongs, obviously, in the category of nonfiction, and from it we expect, certainly, honesty as well as candor and fidelity to historical and biographical truth, in addition to accuracy of representation (the minor flap over Sam Pickering's massaging of the truth for artistic effect—in an early essay on box turtles, this source for *Dead Poets Society* purporting to be a lonely bachelor—witnesses to both readers' expectations and writers' obligation and responsibility). Yet now we refer to the essay as an instance of "creative nonfiction," something of a paradox itself, by which we mean that while *generally* adhering to literal truth, the essay feels free to use all sorts of *literary* and fictional devices to achieve an end having more to do with the integrity and demands of the work than with the strictest adherence to facts and concerns of verisimilitude. Of course, some essayists—Pickering among them—actively exploit the creative potential of the form, working at the boundaries of essay and fiction (he frequently tells tall tales and creates "local color" characters without crossing the line into the short story, sometimes a fine distinction). In the protean essay, the letter and the spirit sleep together, sometimes uneasily and fitfully, sometimes quite comfortably.

The truth of the matter is, the best works best—fulfilling its destiny, as Lukács would say—when its inevitable and unavoidable tension is readily acknowledged and exploited. I mean, the most satisfying and successful essays are not those closest to the memoir or the confession, but rather where the essayist reins in his individualistic, self-assertive, and self-expressive tendencies and makes something—paradoxically enough—unique. Who prefers Nancy Mairs's blatant and embarrassing admissions of marital infidelity to E. B. White's dramatization of sensibility, penitence, and humility ("Death of a Pig" may be exemplary)? When Edward Hoagland writes crisply and cleanly about "city walking," black bears, and boxing, we embrace the familiar voice and like and respect the man; but we withhold this admiration when he reveals too much about himself (for instance, spanking a girlfriend with a hair brush).

Although the distinction nowadays is rarely observed, a difference exists between the personal essay and the familiar. Whereas the personal leans often perilously close to memoir, the familiar essay—whose exemplars include Chesterton, his friend Belloc, Woolf, White, and most recently, Joseph Epstein and Anne Fadiman—represents the self not for its own sake but rather as a crucible in which experience is tried and tested. As indicated in titles frequently beginning "On" or "Of," familiar essays may or may not be lighter in tone (as Lopate suggests), a mere *jeu d'esprit* or "sublimated chatter" (Hartman). They *are* "about" something, and with the self as medium—rather than the message—familiar essays proceed in *a posteriori* and inductive fashion to make a generalizable point of some significance: "Of Books," "On Being a Cripple" (Mairs), "On Morality" (Didion), "Nature" (Emerson), "Walking" (Thoreau), "Shooting an Elephant" (Orwell), "Death of the Moth" (Woolf), "The Ring of Time" (White). In familiar essays, the "I" is not the subject; the subject is, instead, outside and other than the self, public rather than private, social or cultural instead of individual. The self explores, remembers, reflects, and assays but is not stroked or aggrandized; sometimes it is laid bare in its pettiness and pride.

I APPROACH CONCLUSION by returning to Eliot, specifically his great essay "Tradition and the Individual Talent." No clearer example may exist of the issues we have been tracing. This essay does more, however, than offer thematic statements regarding the nature of poetry and the relation of those two (willful) forces represented in its title. (The coordinate conjunction here does not lack for significance.)

A critical essay, "Tradition and the Individual Talent" is familiar but certainly not personal. The "I" appears, but sparingly; characteristic of Eliot's writing here and elsewhere is the use of both first-person plural and second-person ("we" is, in fact, the essay's fourth word), which militates against the kind of (pseudo) objectivity found in the (definite) article. It would be unfair to call this essay impersonal; it does not, in other words, match manner to matter in arguing for an "Impersonal theory of poetry." It "hangs between" the article and the personal essay, extremes that it avoids. At the same time, it is hard to miss the tension in Eliot's definite opposition to Wordsworth, in his submission of a revolutionary view of poetry directed against the earlier, Romantic revolution, and in his not-entirely-traditional interpretation of the individual's alteration of tradition even as he "surrenders" to it. The essay's tension recalls the tension in *Religio Laici*: Eliot too, although he never says so directly, accepts the revolution that ushered in "the autonomy of the private individual," then seeks to redirect it, back toward the very tradition it overthrew and now generally flouts. Eliot's argument in "Tradition and the Individual Talent" thus mirrors the situation of the essay, as essayists accepted the bequest of Montaigne.

The unavoidable tension involved is readily apparent when Eliot writes, "Poetry is not a turning loose of emotion, but an escape from emotion; it is not the expression of personality, but an escape from personality. But, of course, only those who have personality and emotions know what it means to want to escape from these things."[22] The prose is familiar, not personal, Baconian rather than Montaignian—and it is not that of the purely impersonal article, either. Work must be done, moreover, which means restraint and discipline, itself an acknowledgement of tension. Surrender never removes the tension, because the effort is ongoing, continuous. We can see now why Eliot regards penitence and humility as "the foundation of the Christian life," arguing for them when he waxes most personal, for temptation is ever present.[23] As Jeanette Winterson says, Eliot, like the poets he admires most, is a poet of great feeling "but tightly kept." As you read "Tradition and the Individual Talent," you feel the emotion as well as the temptation being resisted, personality and individuality held in check yet powerful. What provides the necessary counterforce appears strikingly in the essay's last sentence. The penultimate word carries the burden of the thought, incarnating the surrender Eliot describes as necessary in the poet—that tradition persists and prevails even *without the "individual talent"* puts the aspirant in his place: "And he is not likely to know what is to be done unless he lives in what is not merely the present, but the present moment of the past, unless he is conscious, not of what is dead, but of what is already living."[24] With another paradox, Eliot thus concludes perhaps his most important essay. At its best, his prose is a coiled spring, full of feeling, energy, and tension.

I ONCE THOUGHT of "the essayistic spirit" as if it were an airy and ethereal thing that hovered just above the page or apart from the essayist as he struggles to pen a thing unpretentious and humble, artful and personal, exploratory and undogmatic. The truth, I now realize, lies elsewhere. The essay is actually a thing of the letter, its spirit incarnate in and inseparable from its material basis. The essay both grounds and roots us, reminding us of ties to place and to our very physical, everyday existence. It helps prevent us from flying "by those nets" flung at the soul "to hold it back from flight" (Stephen Dedalus). The essay materializes and it familiarizes, bringing us down from the heavens to the earth, from the imagination to reality, from too much thought to our sensuous and sensual nature to where we belong, "hanging between," neither quite a god nor merely a beast. We are a fallible, needy, but at our best intelligent and sympathetic Don Pedro de Mendez, neither Houyhnhnm nor Yahoo.

Such recognition humbles, making the essay the thesis behind the antithesis that is satire (though often included in essay collections such as Fakundiny's, Swift's "A Modest Proposal" is actually a satire that is essayistic only in its thesis passage offering an alternative to cannibalism). A note of caution, anyway, must accompany Lukács's widely accepted argument regarding the essay's "characteristic" irony: he comes dangerously close to flouting the form's modesty in claiming that, despite appearances, it aims for "the Ultimate." If this be so, it is only in, through, and by means of those supposedly inessential and superficial details that constitute its *raison d'être*. A certain delicacy attends the essay, rendering descriptions of it problematic. I think Lukács overstates its seriousness, its ambition, its worth, a vestige of Romantic assertiveness nearly Promethean in texture.

I will end with a brief look at G. K. Chesterton's essay "A Piece of Chalk," which clarifies and extends my own rather large claims concerning the essay's preference for the letter rather than the spirit. Now, this particular piece exemplifies the essay's way of beginning with the small and then showing it fraught with large implications, as Chesterton moves out to matters of aesthetics and religion, finally to a statement about England as "a tradition and a civilization."[25]

This essay tries too hard, takes on too much, overstepping the fine line that separates it from the sermon (Eliot's little-known *Sermon*, which I have cited above, makes no such mistake, for its claims are more modest, and it actually succeeds as essay better than Chesterton's essay). But before we get to Chesterton's tendentious reflections on whiteness and virtue and a rather smug declaration of "the best religious morality, of real Christianity for example," we are treated to some fine writing about drawing—the fine writing very nearly seduces. But then we stop just short of agreement, for Chesterton leaves the earthly foundation of the essay to fly above and away with the disembodied soul:

> Do not, for heaven's sake, imagine I was going to sketch from Nature. I was going to draw devils and seraphim, and blind old gods that man worshipped before the dawn of right, and saints in robes of angry crimson, and seas of strange green, and all the sacred or monstrous symbols that look so well in bright colours on brown paper. They are much better worth drawing than Nature; also they are much easier to draw. When a cow came slouching by in the field

> next to me, a mere artist might have drawn it; but I always get wrong in the hind legs of quadrapeds. So I drew the soul of the cow; which I saw there plainly walking before me in the sunlight; and the soul was all purple and silver, and had seven horns and the mystery that belongs to all the beasts. But though I could not with a crayon get the best out of the landscape, it does not follow that the landscape was not getting the best out of me.

I detect the slightest hint of Chesterton's awareness he has gone too far (he says, of pre-Romantic poets, who did care for nature although "they did not describe it much," that "They gave out much less about Nature, but they drank in, perhaps, much more").[26]

Robert Browning's great poem "Fra Lippo Lippi" is apposite, helping us to grasp Chesterton's embrace of mere transcendentalism. Whereas in the poem the Prior's represented requirement is, like the poet's, to "lift [men] over it, ignore it all, / Make them forget there's such a thing as flesh. Your business," the fun-loving monk says he was told, "is to paint the souls of men" (181–83).[27] Fra Lippo knows better. Counter to the Prior's Chestertonian injunction to "Paint the soul, never mind the legs and arms!" (193), he speaks essayistically, true to Christianity: "The world's no blot for us, / Nor blank; it means intensely, and means good: / To find its meaning is my meat and drink" (313–15). Indeed, Fra Lippo declares, sarcastically, "A fine way to paint soul, by painting body / So ill, the eye can't stop there, must go further / And can't fare worse" (199–201). The true path, he insists, is *through* the body: "Make his flesh liker and his soul more like, / Both in their order" (207–8). Soul you find, therefore, in and through the surrounding beauty, including that inside yourself when "you return [God] thanks"

(220). The decidedly unorthodox painter thus restores balance that escapes the supposedly orthodox Chesterton.

Obviously, Chesterton prefers to look through rather than at Nature. Looking through Nature would be fine, if one meant what Chesterton does not, and that is, looking *by means of*. My (Eliotesque) point is that you can't reach the soul directly, but only through the body, the letter. Not being able to abide such tension and in such an "in-between" state, Dryden wrote, after his conversion to Roman Catholicism, *The Hind and the Panther*, a very spiritual poem, altogether different in texture from his apologia for the *via media*.

FORM AND MEANING
THE ESSAY'S IMMANENT PURPOSIVENESS

The critic of forms ... conceives purpose as an immanent or indwelling rather than transcendent cause. He holds the connection between purpose and structure to be direct and continuous: rather than locating purpose in a disembodied realm of general artistic ends or abstract intentions, he strives to find it at work in the dynamic progression of the text.

Walter A. Davis, *The Act of Interpretation: A Critique of Literary Reason*

Immanent Form

FORM IS NOT MEANING. To say so is tempting, and perhaps understandable, but it is also to elide difference and enter a dangerous collapse. By the same token, we can say that form is *not* "not meaning." Further, we can say this: without form meaning does not exist. In, through, and by means of form meaning is realized.

If we take form as like a transcendent power, existing beyond and apart from the work of art, an abstract, Gnostic-like category, we commit an injustice no less serious than when we ignore, dismiss, or minimize the importance of form, impatient with the concrete. Impatience rules in any case, from the hasty, even rapacious shift from concrete details to meaning, to the equally quick and reckless refusal to be bothered with meaning. The truth is, we cannot do without either form or meaning; one without the other is an impoverishment, and more, a distortion as well as a failure of imagination and understanding. I say "truth" because incarnation reveals the pattern that opens understanding: *embodied* truth.

Form is something notoriously difficult to grasp. I can never seem to get hold of it, let alone pin it down. Perhaps Plato is to blame, locating it far from us in some ideal realm and thus promoting error. It is better—not just easier, but truer—to regard form as inseparable from purpose and purposiveness, as Walter A. Davis argues in *The Act of Interpretation*:

> Put in the simplest and most exacting terms, the task of interpretation is to apprehend the purposive principle immanent in the

> structure of a literary work which determines the mutual interfunctioning of its component parts. . . . Function, structure, and purpose, in that order, become the primary categories of interpretation: for parts function only by serving a purpose and structure is the process through which purpose is actualized. . . . Purpose coincides with structure because it gives birth to it. It is the most concrete category in criticism because its embodiment is constant and comprehensive: the purpose that shapes a work of art is realized by no more and no less than that entire work of art.

Such an understanding brings form down from the ethereal and the ideal and places it, surprisingly enough, within the ordinary and the concrete—for the student of literature, *in* the text rather than outside, above, and beyond it, hovering, untouchable, and controlling. To think of form as immanent is by no means to equate it with meaning, but rather with purpose and purposiveness—which is to leave meaning alone altogether. No less than form, meaning, too, appears susceptible to the same sort of disembodiment whereby we conceive of it as existing apart or at least separable from the work itself, lying, for instance, in the author's abstract intention. This tendency accounts, I imagine, for the not-so-sophomoric drive to yank meaning from the work of literature and place it, somehow summarized, encapsulated, and rendered free of all the writer's fripperies and the reader's window dressing, in a simple paraphrased unit, boiled down, we say, put in a nutshell, thus reduced to and presented as *content*.

THE ESSAY IS NEITHER shapeless nor formless, although it resists our vaunted attempts to describe or define that form. We talk as if the essay is at once a form and without one. The species "essay" may, in other words, *be* a form, but individual instances of that form lack form. Various inconsistencies and contradictions thus attach to this resistant, defiant thing to which we keep returning and that we apparently love unconditionally.

It has been described, crudely enough, as "a greased pig" and as "a pair of baggy pants into which nearly anything and everything can fit."[1] Authors of such descriptions intend not to demean the writing to which they themselves are given—and with which they are often smitten. Faced with describing the form, they are reduced to homely analogies, thereby, I'm afraid, reducing the form itself. They decline, in any case, to go so far as to conclude that the essay is a mere lump. It may be a parti-colored quilt, as I once proposed, made of scraps and remnants, or at least appearing so, but it amounts to more than random thoughts, bits, and pieces carelessly assembled or merely cobbled together. The essay cannot be equated with, or reduced to, unfettered self-expression, the directionless ramblings of a wanderer out for an idle stroll. Reasons for drawing these conclusions are, however, manifold: from the titles of periodical publications like the *Spectator*, the *Tatler*, and the *Idler* to essayists' own penchant for writing about libertarian strolls in the south of England and Unnamed Pond near Storrs, Connecticut. Commentators on the essay nowadays, myself included, exude their delight in finding and having a form so deconfining and capacious; we cannot but extol its virtues as distinct from the narrowness and impersonality of the writing so many of us are expected to produce. Like many others, I find the essay an engaging, attractive Other.

In the essay, which can lay no claim to peculiarity in the matter, form indwells. The essay, in other words, is no more formless than any other writing. Each essay has shape as well, although that form is immanent. As an example, consider Scott Russell Sanders's popular "Under the Influence," which first appeared in *Harper's*, was then included in his collection *Secrets of the Universe*, and later was anthologized in Lopate's *The Art of the Personal Essay*. I choose this instance because "Under the Influence" might seem to represent a particularly strong case against my argument. Indeed, its very manner would appear to militate against any sense of structure as "the continuous manifestation and development of an organizing purpose."

Broken into nine sections, each separated by extra white space, the essay complicates and perhaps problematizes my drive, and Walter A. Davis's, to locate textual integrity and purposive movement. In Sanders's essay, the greatest obstacle to locating immanent form appears early. After a strong and effective opening section rendered with powerful and moving images, the essayist seems to pause, interrupting the purposive movement apparently underway to "consider a few of our synonyms for *drunk*." This linguistic foray leads to imagined representations of those men who, like his oft-besotted father, fell "under the influence" of demon rum. Yet that pathetic father enters here, and Sanders returns to the strong language that, in fact, he never swerved from, only applied differently: the essay's hook—"My father drank"—modulates into "There seemed to be a leak in him somewhere," the brief linguistic excursus now appearing as an integral part of the reflection underway.[2]

Sanders told me once that, in effect, he had no conception of an essay's organic growth as he wrote, writing being, instead, a matter of assembling, in proper order, some separately wrought pieces—not unlike the making of a quilt, I reckon, or Annie Dillard's description of her act of composition in *The Writing Life*. The forceful separation of Sanders's essay into distinct though related units accentuates our initial sense of the lack of purposive movement, which we thought was also present in Hazlitt's "On Going a Journey." The next section of "Under the Influence" seems to confirm this perception, if not of randomness, then at least of a "progression" based only on the mind wandering around a topic. And indeed, in pointing to and often extolling the essay's rambling nature, commentators suggest, however inadvertently, that its elusive and protean character is little more than a working draft. Theodor Adorno, for one, applauds this "genuine" movement of thinking (as opposed to thought) because it represents, he says, a mind liberal and free of "administrative" seductions. Edward Hoagland more approachably describes a personal essay as "like the human voice talking, its order the mind's natural flow, instead of a systematized outline of ideas. . . . [I]t conveys," he concludes, "the quality of the author's mind."[3] To be sure, but how? Directly, through what Hoagland calls its "tumbling progression"? Or indirectly, by means of the writer's control and shaping of experience *cum* reflection? I am inclined to think Jeanette Winterson near the mark when she writes, in *Art Objects: Essays on Ecstasy and Effrontery*, that "The bad writer believes that sincerity of feeling will be enough, and pins her faith on the power of experience. The true writer knows that feeling must give way to form. It is through the form," she concludes, "not in spite of, or accidental to it, that the most powerful emotions are let loose over the greatest number of people."[4] I can imagine no more compelling apologia for form, which Winterson, like Virginia Woolf before her, establishes as the opposite of mere self-expression.

Form prevails in "Under the Influence" as well, despite appearances. What has already begun to appear is the essay's true focus not on his father but on Scott himself. He finds himself caught between his alcoholic father and his own ten-year-old son, worrying that, as a workaholic, he is repeating—and bequeathing to his son—a sad and dangerous pattern. Sanders begins to establish this focus even in the opening section, although I did not, and perhaps could not, appreciate it until I read on. The shift to the present does more than more closely involve the reader by creating immediacy; it places the story of his father's alcoholism in the present moment of the essayist and his world. Thus:

> I am forty-two as I write these words, and I know full well now that my father was an alcoholic, a man consumed by desire rather than by disappointment.... There are keener sources of grief: poverty, racism, rape, war. I do not wish to compete for a trophy in suffering. I am only trying to understand the corrosive mixture of helplessness, responsibility, and shame that I learned to feel as the son of an alcoholic. I realize now that I did not cause my father's illness, nor could I have cured it. Yet for all this grown-up knowledge, I am still ten years old, my own son's age, and as that boy I struggle in guilt and confusion to save my father from pain.[5]

Sanders has also said that he writes in order to try to solve a problem; "Under the Influence" functions as a journey to understanding—its true form.

The reflections that follow represent, therefore, much more than random thoughts; they also function as something more and other than a window onto the essayist's mind at work. In truth, Sanders's reflections are stations of this pilgrim's progress: the battles that incriminated his stealthy father, their power and their source; the drunkards in the neighborhood and in the Bible, which so colored understanding; the devastating effects of drinking in other families as well as Sanders's; the hopes ever rising but always dashed of change; the end of the quest for perfection and the ensuing determination. The demons left over and bequeathed to him constitute Sanders's focus and the essay's problem, which he tries to come to grips with. The penultimate section moves toward a conclusion with these powerful reflections:

> Life with him and the loss of him twisted us into shapes that will be familiar to other sons and daughters of alcoholics. My brother became a rebel, my sister retreated into shyness, I played the stalwart and dutiful son who would hold the family together. If my father was unstable, I would be a rock. If he squandered money on drink, I would pinch every penny. If he wept when drunk—and only when drunk—I would not let myself weep at all. If he roared at the Little League umpire for calling my pitches balls, I would throw nothing but strikes. Watching him flounder and rage, I came to dread the loss of control. I would go through life without making anyone mad.

Control is the point, and Sanders is forming his life in a way that his writing reflects—he would not, could not, fashion it of mere self-expression, a shapeless random movement, however well intentioned.

> I vowed never to put in my mouth or veins any chemical that would banish my everyday self. I would never make a scene, never lash out at the ones I loved, never hurt a soul. Through hard work, relentless work, I would achieve something dazzling—in the classroom, on the basketball floor, in the science lab, in the pages of books—and my achievement would distract the world's eyes from his humilia-

tion. I would become a worthy sacrifice, and the smoke of my burning would please God.[6]

Here speaks the essayistic voice of nonviolence, mode and manner mirroring each other perfectly: there is none of the competitiveness, one-upmanship, martial imagery, or desire to win that characterizes "that awful object, 'the article.'"[7]

But the story is not yet finished, for no effort, however determined and courageous, brings redemption. Thus Sanders edges his account closer and closer to the present moment, his real concern:

> It is far easier to recognize these twists in my character than to undo them. Work has become an addiction for me, as drink was an addiction for my father. Knowing this, my daughter gave me a placard for the wall: WORKAHOLIC. The labor is endless and futile, for I can no more redeem myself through work than I could redeem my father. I still panic in the face of other people's anger, because his drunken temper was so terrible. I shrink from causing sadness or disappointment even to strangers, as though I were still concealing the family shame. I still notice every twitch of emotion in the faces around me, having learned as a child to read the weather in faces, and I blame myself for the least pang of unhappiness or anger. In certain moods I blame myself for everything. Guilt burns like acid in my veins.[8]

Rather than confessional in spirit, this writing is honest self-evaluation. Sanders has, indeed, traveled far in his journey: from difference from his father, to close similarity (perhaps identity), and finally to sympathy.

Turning in the brief final section to his son, Sanders notes that he repeats the pattern that he himself has found operating in the story of him and his own father. His son, writes Sanders, is already "taking on himself the griefs of the world, and in particular the griefs of his father. He tells me that when I am gripped by sadness he feels responsible; he feels there must be something he can do to spring me from depression, to fix my life." He thus repeats exactly what Scott felt and did in a different but structurally identical situation. "I write, therefore," says Sanders, "to drag into the light what eats at me—the fear, the guilt, the shame—so that my own children may be spared."[9] So saying, he at last differentiates himself from his father, this time on the basis of love.

As to the drink that consumed his father's life and menaces still his own and that of his family, Sanders says that he shies away from occasions "where the solvent is alcohol." He admits to tasting alcohol first at twenty-one, but "I sipped warily." He then ends with these words, perhaps a representation of mediated freedom: "I still do—once a week, perhaps, a glass of wine, a can of beer, nothing stronger, nothing more. I listen for the turning of a key in my brain."[10] Having less control, I drank more than Sanders and actually heard that key turning; having stopped in time, I know exactly whereof Sanders writes. And write well he does, because "Under the Influence" is carefully shaped, very nearly chiseled. Its meaning—which defies easy summary—is inseparable from its form. Shape *is*, after all, what the essay is all about, life and art reflecting each other.

Embodied Truth

E. B. White's justly famous "Death of a Pig" complicates matters with regards to the voice, that is, to the "speaker" and his truth-bearing, and it requires a distinction unnecessary in discussing "Under the Influence." Time in this essay reveals form as dependent upon one who, unlike Sanders, cannot sustain the burden of his textual responsibility. That incapacity is not moral but is instead a failure of total form. In that failure, "Death of a Pig" points to the locus of truth in the essay as form. No *Animal Farm*, this essay nevertheless has interest in big game, as the second and third paragraphs establish. These paragraphs also reinforce our intuition of tension, because the story and moral truth do not run on the same timeline. Indeed, time has already entered the equation, for White has noted how he feels "driven to account for this stretch of time" during which he cared for his ailing pig: "the pig died at last, and I lived, and things might easily have gone the other way round and none left to do the accounting." In the event of the "accounting," this writing, White confesses that he "cannot recall the hours sharply," nor is he able to say "how many nights I had sat up with a pig," nor indeed "whether death came on the third night or the fourth night." This inability, this uncertainty rocks his mental world and afflicts him "with a sense of personal deterioration."[11] Thus "Death of a Pig" is fully as much about White as it is about the unnamed pig, unlucky victim.

The second and third paragraphs of White's essay introduce the major metaphors of performance, drama, tragedy, and farce. What appears earlier in the essay as farce is described here as tragedy, although White complicates even this. Here are these remarkable sentences:

> The scheme of buying a spring pig in blossomtime, feeding it through summer and fall, and butchering it when the solid cold weather arrives, is a familiar scheme to me and follows an antique pattern. It is a tragedy enacted on most farms with perfect fidelity

to the original script. The murder, being premeditated, is in the first degree but is quick and skillful, and the smoked bacon and ham provide a ceremonial ending whose fitness is seldom questioned.

White's position is clearly ambiguous; it *appears*, for instance, that the play is a tragedy only for the pig—it alone ends unhappily. In the writing, then, White's sympathies are already with his pig, the only unnamed character in this "play." He begins to explain the reason for his sympathy in the immediately following sentences:

> Once in a while something slips—one of the actors goes up in his lines and the whole performance stumbles and halts. My pig simply failed to show up for a meal. The alarm spread rapidly. The classic outline of the tragedy was lost. I found myself cast suddenly in the role of pig's friend and physician—a farcical character with an enema bag for a prop. I had a presentiment, the very first afternoon, that the play would never regain its balance and that my sympathies were now wholly with the pig. This was slapstick—the sort of dramatic treatment that instantly appealed to my old dachshund, Fred, who joined the vigil, held the bag, and when all was over, presided at the interment. When we slid the body into the grave, we both were shaken to the core. The loss we felt was not the loss of ham but the loss of pig. He had evidently become precious to me, not that he represented a distant nourishment in a hungry time, but that he had suffered in a suffering world. But I'm running ahead of my story and shall have to go back.[12]

White's world has indeed become upset. It has turned upside down, in fact, and his apparent lack of narrative control mirrors that disturbance as it complicates our apprehension of "structure as the continuous manifestation and development of an organizing purpose." Aristotle's neat conception of the world is thus compromised, at the very least.

Since we know the outcome of the pig's travails, our attention is on neither the plot nor that character but on his caretaker (as well, of course, as on the delightful humor). White disguises or withholds none of his desires:

> I sank into a chair and sat still for a few minutes to think about *my* troubles, and then I got up and went to the barn, catching up on some odds and ends that needed tending to. Unconsciously I held off, for an hour, the dread by which I would officially recognize the collapse of the performance of raising a pig; I wanted no interruption in the regularity of feeding, the steadiness of growth, the even succession of days. I wanted no interruption, wanted no oil, no deviation. I just wanted to keep on raising a pig, full meal after full meal, spring into summer into fall.[13]

At the time, then, White's concern is primarily *his* troubles, and he seems at this point to worry less about the pig's suffering and more about his failure to perform successfully his duty, that "collapse of the performance of raising a pig."

A bit later, White understands the pig's misfortune primarily as pointing to the precariousness and transience of his own state, to *him*. The pig he does not (yet) recognize as pig, and so cannot understand or sympathize with him.

> At this point, although a depression had settled over me, I didn't suppose that I was going to lose my pig. From the lustiness of a healthy pig a man derives a feeling of personal lustiness; the stuff

that goes into the trough and is received with such enthusiasm is an earnest of some later feast of his own, and when this suddenly comes to an end and the food lies stale and untouched, souring in the sun, the pig's imbalance becomes the man's, vicariously, and life seems insecure, displaced, transitory.

But then a change occurs after he and Fred have administered an enema of warm suds to the suffering pig. "I discovered," says White,

> that once having given a pig an enema there is no turning back, no chance of resuming one of life's stereotyped roles. The pig's lot and mine were inextricably bound now, as though the rubber tube were the silver cord. From then until the time of his death I held the pig steadily in the bowl of my mind; the task of trying to deliver him from his misery became a strong obsession. His suffering soon *became the embodiment of all earthly wretchedness.*[14] (Italics added)

Humor, sometimes grim, exists alongside the developing sense of suffering—and perhaps of tragedy in quite another, more capacious fashion than that earlier.

As the pig's condition persists and in fact worsens, White becomes all the more aware of the tenuousness of his own world. His and the pig's lot appear all the more bound together, but despite his feeling, White remains self-absorbed. The story of the pig points still to him: it is *he* for whom the pig's suffering matters; the bell may toll for his charge, but it is he who hears it and in so doing imagines himself as the subject. No amount of humor or wit or brilliant narration can hide or disguise the fact. *Our* sympathies lie more with the pig than do White's, more with the pig, in fact, than with the hypochondriacal White, who is no Eumaios the faithful swineherd (but more a Phaiacian perhaps succored on Circe's potions):

> My throat felt dry and I went to the cupboard and got a bottle of whiskey. . . . I had assumed that there could be nothing much wrong with a pig during the months it was being groomed for murder; my confidence in the essential health and endurance of pigs had been strong and deep, particularly in the health of pigs that belonged to me and that were part of my proud scheme. The awakening had been violent and I minded it all the more because I knew that what could be true of my pig could be true also of the rest of my tidy world. I tried to put this distasteful idea from me, but it kept recurring. I took a short drink of the whiskey and then, although I wanted to go down to the yard and look for fresh signs, I was scared to. I was certain that I had erysipelas.[15]

By now, the essayist's conclusion is predictable in the same way the pig's death is inevitable. White has failed to learn, failed to take true advantage of the opportunity—or at least the essay's "voice" has:

> I have written this account in penitence and in grief, as a man who failed to raise his pig, and to explain my deviation from the classic course of so many raised pigs. The grave in the woods is unmarked, but Fred can direct the mourner to it unerringly and with immense good will, and I know he and I shall often revisit it, singly and together, in seasons of reflection and despair, on flagless memorial days of our own choosing.[16]

Where does White stand in all of this, White the essayist that is, the biographical figure outside the text? Do we equate him with the so-called persona or voice here? Or is that voice created, fictive? Perhaps you will say that I have overread this slight *jeu d'esprit*—after all, I too enjoy ham and bacon, the fruits of what "White" insists on calling murder. Perhaps I have, although I would respond that I seek only to follow the essay's purposive movement.

In every sense I can think of, Elwyn Brooks White is the subject of "Death of a Pig"—at least, the subject is the White who appears *in* the essay. That figure, persona, or represented author does not, as I read it, embody the values to which I subscribe. I am left wondering, then—which may testify to the work's enduring power. However that may be, this unresolved tension means that I cannot with confidence say who in the text embodies the truth. Certainly the speaker of "Death of a Pig" does not, unless it be that he "becomes the embodiment of all earthly" tension, tension in which we all are caught, to be sure. At the very least, though, White's essay points to the crucial importance to the form of the speaker, especially as he or she functions to embody the work's principal values. Whether or not it fulfils that function tells, but does not ruin this essay as art.

FORM SEEMS MORE IMPORTANT to an essay when it is clearly and directly processual in nature, like Sanders's "Under the Influence." In such essays, the writer voyages to understanding in, through, and by means of the writing—a true essay, one is tempted to say, an attempt to learn. Of course, it is possible to simulate such discovery. At any rate, when the essayist already rests in possession of truth, knowing it from word one, then *immanent form* slides over into *embodied truth*. Form recedes but never disappears; on the contrary, it often appears as the embodiment of truth. The difference, hardly sophistical, is subtle and important.

I instance once more Hilaire Belloc's marvelous essay "The Mowing of a Field." With engaging descriptions of the south of England around the turn into the twentieth century, the essay appears to resist all or nearly all that the terrible time to come would bear witness to. It begins slowly, patiently, and unpretentiously, and that is precisely the point, as we learn in moving with the essay from this loving account of Belloc's return to his physical and emotional home after years away, thence to his account of resuming the richly implicated art of mowing, and finally to a concluding pair of stories detailing the respectful and traditional ways of living in this isolated but not-Phaiacia-like part of England's green and glorious land. You don't hurry—if you do, you pay a considerable price.

Mowing is an art, not a science, neither a chore nor a pastime. You have to know how to do it, just as you must know when the grass is ready and how to sharpen the scythe for the fit work. As to the latter, Belloc writes lovingly, passionately about this mundane activity too, for meaning lies in it. That art, he begins, "is worth describing fully," which he proceeds to do in a fashion by no means technical and addressed to the second-person since this is all very much a personal matter. The instruction given, the preparation done, the skill achieved if not yet perfected as art; you are now ready for the appreciation awaiting you—the measurement musical, not numerical:

> To tell when the scythe is sharp enough this is the rule. First the stone clangs and grinds against the iron harshly; then it rings musically to one note; then, at last, it purrs as though the iron and stone were exactly suited. When you hear this, your scythe is sharp enough; and I, when I heard it that June dawn, with everything

quite silent except the birds, let down the scythe and bent myself to mow.[17]

Bent to mow, Belloc appears, if not in a position of genuflection and supplication, certainly in an act of reverence and obeisance.

Time is a subject here, as it is in "Under the Influence"—as it is in perhaps all essays. In Sanders's essay, reflection on the past serves to enlighten and possibly to unburden the present; in "The Mowing of a Field," differently, the past lives on in the present, its virtues passed down and kept intact. Arguably, time constitutes the essay's—the form's—true subject matter: not just what to do with it, as if in a retirement mode, but how to cope with and understand its ravages. E. B. White's essays treat nothing else: not just in "The Ring of Time" but also in "Death of a Pig," "Once More to the Lake," and "What Do Our Hearts Treasure?," where space functions as time. Concerned with the present in whatever manner, essays reflect the present's supreme value, creatures of immanence that find meaning and truth, here and now.

For Belloc, tradition connects present with past, endowing the present with meaning and acting as resistance. The past is a moral reminder, a call to truth. Belloc rises to eloquence, the shape and texture of his sentences embodying a voice that is impassioned and truth-telling; he sometimes resembles the Old Testament prophet who reminds, recalls, and rebukes. In this instance, the bad mower thus reenacts an ancient pattern, the antagonist in a tragic drama. He causes the meadow to bleed because he repeats the pattern of haste, disrespect, and violence present *"depuis la fondation du monde."*

But the good mower who does things just as they should be done and have been for a hundred thousand years, falls into none of these fooleries. He goes forward very steadily, his scythe-blade just barely missing the ground, every grass falling; the swish and rhythm of his mowing are always the same.[18]

Belloc lacks the pretension and arrogance—no Promethean, he—to suggest that mowing is an allegory (although I suspect he is aware of the tradition in Renaissance English literature of "mower" poems, themselves representations, willy-nilly, of Christ). And yet mowing shares with other activities certain unsurpassable values; it participates, no meaner or richer than any other, in the range of human endeavor, every act of which deserves respect and bears significance. Mowing is no more a metaphor for writing than writing is for mowing; they may or may not be equal in some scheme of importance that, in any case, man is incapable of ascertaining. Mowing and writing sit alongside one another, alike in the structure Belloc invokes: they instance work, neither of them (as he suggests elsewhere regarding writing) "creative" but, more modestly, both developmental, a matter of cultivating a germ that owes its existence to a power other and greater than man. The Catholic, even anti-Protestant, nature of these described activities points up the tension ever present in the essay as form.

The concluding paragraphs of "The Mowing of a Field" disturb or, better, disconcert many readers, who have trouble linking to the foregoing the representation of the buying and selling of labor, pig, and land. Ostensibly, of course, Belloc is narrating his day's activity, which proceeds through the perfecting of his scythe, thence to mowing, and finally to the unexpected arrival of a swarthy man from beyond the valley seeking work. What links this account and the succeeding, briefer tale of a man buying land to the art of mowing is actually soon made clear. Bargaining, too, is an art, although of a somewhat different kind, but it is structurally alike in its ethical basis; here comedy replaces tragedy. Tradition dictates a way of patience and respect that necessarily entails a detour. For everywhere, the Valley flourishes and experiences joy and wonder because, under no illusion about reality and truth, it adds *flesh* to "the dry bones of commerce, avarice and method and need," making "a pretty *body* of fiction and observances" (italics added). Such embodiment bears the name of art.[19]

In the Valley, haste is violence, as it is in art. I quote a remarkable paragraph near the end of "The Mowing of a Field" that rounds out these themes, as well as the manner, and succinctly delivers the truth that has for some time been made familiar:

> Thus do we buy a pig or land or labour or malt or lime, always with elaboration and set forms; and many a London man has paid double and more for his violence and his greedy haste and very unchilvarous higgling. As happened with the land at Underwaltham, which the mortgagees had begged and implored the estate to take at twelve hundred, and had privately offered to all the world at a thousand, but which a sharp *direct* man, of the kind that makes great fortunes, a man in a motor-car, a man in a fur coat, *a man of few words*, bought for two thousand three hundred before my very eyes, protesting that they might take his offer or leave it; and all because he did not begin by praising the land.[20] (Italics added)

Belloc began, of course, by doing just that.

In this essay, unlike "Death of a Pig," I never worry about a difference or discrepancy between speaker and author (the widest difference I know of in a so-called essay occurs in Swift's wildly satirical "A Modest Proposal"). The speaker in "The Mowing of a Field" is to be identified with Hilaire Belloc—it is he, in fact. And it is he who embodies the touted values of patience and respect. In embodying truth, the truth the essay is built upon and advocates, Belloc—for so we may as well call the "speaker"—stands forth as our best access to it, a perhaps necessary mediation, in any case the modal point at which, I am inclined to conclude, transcendence intersects with, or crosses, immanence. He makes concrete and human the values, the truth, represented in the various accounts narrated and described.

In Belloc, *embodied truth* becomes *immanent form*: form, which is the same thing as truth, is fleshed out and represented in a person. Belloc's good friend Chesterton may have been unable, or so he claims in "A Piece of Chalk," to see through creatures to the form they embody, but Belloc leaves no doubt about his incarnationism—his orthodoxy.

IN-BETWEENNESS
THE BURDEN OF THE ESSAY

—

"... almost *literature and* almost *philosophy*."
Eduardo Nicol

—

THE IDEA of the essay as embodied truth, which I advanced in the preceding chapter, is important because it qualifies the familiar stress on voice, defining what has been merely assumed while reducing a certain problematic. "Embodied truth" is a term at once more specific and more inclusive than the deconstructed notion of "voice," which is attended by complications and simplicities. My notion does more, I believe, pointing to the essay's significance. The various terms I have used here—not only "embodied truth" but also, for instance, "incarnate form" and even *via media*—are highly charged, but unavoidable. In this chapter I try to make explicit what has so far been only implied.

I begin the effort by considering the essay's relation to other literary forms. I do so by means of the central notions we have located: experience and meaning. The essay's particular *via media* position is too little appreciated. Here, I will extend my earlier reflections on the tension that marks the essay, its in-betweenness.

William H. Gass has famously defined the essay's relation to "the 'definite' article": professional or scholarly writing is, he allows, "the opposite" of the form Montaigne bequeathed to us. The essay's relation to the novel is, of course, readily acknowledged, particularly via the social criticism and treatment of manners in the *Tatler* and the *Spectator*. And recently the essay and the lyric have been associated. Precedent is ample for other associations, given, for example, Pope's versified *An Essay on Criticism* and *An Essay on Man*, Wordsworth's studied reference to his and Coleridge's "lyrical ballads" as "short essays," and Virginia Woolf's attempt in *Between the Acts* to effect an "essay-novel," to cite only three well-known instances. Yet in neither recent commentary on the essay nor older accounts of the spectrum of genres and kinds of discourse appears sustained consideration of the "formless" form's relation to fiction and philosophy.

An obvious way in which the essay differs from the short story, from which it is sometimes hard to distinguish, is too little remarked: in the essay, the speaking voice—to return to that familiar if inadequate notion—extracts the meaning from experience and assays it; in fiction, the reader's role is greater and more profound. In essays, practically without exception ("Death of a Pig" being one) the reader's work stops short of the implied author—a reliable narrator, he can be trusted. This important difference separates and distinguishes Swift's "Modest Proposal" from the essay (even though, as I have mentioned, such an astute reader as Lydia Fakundiny includes this great satire in *The Art of the Essay*). Whereas in fiction the narrator—by no means always reliable—may assay, weigh, and pass judgment on experience, the reader can never take for granted his trustworthiness or reliability. We take the essayist and his narrator or persona, however, to be one and the same—that is why we say the essay belongs in the category "nonfiction," even though the experience there represented is necessarily and inevitably shaped. In essays, the speaker weighs and assesses his experience, pointing to the meaning of it; in fiction, the reader does much or even most of this interpretive work.

The voice we hear in essays—that representation of embodied truth—*is* the experiencing, reflecting, and narrating self. But the subject matter of essays, at least of familiar essays, is something other than the subject, other than that self. The subject matter is not merely the experience either or even the meaning mined from the experience. The subject is, rather, all that is undergone: it is a combination of experience, self, and the meaning and significance ultimately derived and then passed along.

Clearly, on a spectrum involving fiction, philosophy, and the essay, the essay would occupy a middle position, thus:

fiction *the essay* *philosophy*

The essay can be so distinguished precisely because it is not absolutely different from either fiction or philosophy. Because it has something in common with each, without being identical, we can make distinctions: aspects of fiction—by which term I include drama and at least much poetry—function in the essay, most notably its penchant for story and so the appearance of plot and characters. In a similar manner, the essay borrows reflection, analysis, and judgment from philosophy. *Tom Jones*, for instance, is a novel that edges, like much other fiction of the eighteenth century, toward philosophy as it incorporates essays on what amounts to the art of living (you can safely say something similar about the later *Moby Dick* and *Adam Bede*; the philosophy of John Locke, contrariwise, neither embraces nor incorporates fiction, but it is offered as an essay).

What the essay gives us, uniquely I maintain, is *reflection upon experience*, and if reflection is the province of philosophy, experience is that of fiction. This is precisely what makes Richard Selzer's "A Worm from My Notebook" an essay: the story of Ibrahim's fatal experience preceded by a paragraph of profound reflection on writing, without which we would have a (not so good) short story. We may thus begin to flesh out the above triad:

fiction *the essay* *philosophy*
experience *reflection upon experience* *reflection*

Of course, philosophy does more than reflect: its object is meaning, exclusively; fiction, on the other hand, is also concerned with meaning, although meaning is not in the foreground but always subordinate to and derived from experience. Philosophy does sometimes clothe itself in fiction—Carlyle's *Sartor Resartus* springs to mind—but instances are few and generally without great merit. The essay, on the other hand, draws freely from literature, its feet always firmly planted in the fertile soil of human experience; it steadfastly resists the Gnostic temptation to forgo mundane, ordinary, and literal reality for the ethereal world of ideas. Ideas are by no means shunned or ignored, but the essayist travels the familiar path to thought by means of the world, people, books, and events that he or she knows firsthand and directly. There is no immediate jump to what Plato called the ideal. As Eliot reminds us, the name of this process—of indirection, of movement to the world of ideas in, through, and by means of what we all share—is incarnation.

The essayist's is a literal imagination, his eye trained on the letter, on concrete particulars, on details; spirit is something he can and often does reach, but only via the *a posteriori* path that spiritualists, Gnostics, and theorists alike eschew. One of the essay's great, enduring contributions lies just here: in its clear-sightedness and its stubborn refusal to pass too quickly beyond the commonplace. Fittingly, essayist and naturalist Wendell Berry titled a recent collection of his nonfiction *The Art of the Commonplace*. The essayist makes art out of what we might too readily miss, dismiss, or skip over in our haste as well as in a misdirected sense of where meaning exists.

The essay, in fact, focuses on achieved meaning to a greater extent than those other forms we typically call literature; essays foreground meaning along with represented experience. Let the latter overwhelm, and the essay becomes fiction or memoir or autobiography; conversely, let meaning dominate and the essay turns into philosophy or perhaps theology. Thus the essay is a creature of poise, as we have often heard, a thing of composure that, balanced, hangs between.

LET US RETURN to the spectrum on which the essay exists between fiction and philosophy/theology and experience and meaning. Indeed, we can continue to flesh out these distinctions and with them the particular place that the essay occupies.

fiction	*the essay*	*philosophy*
experience		*meaning*
word/flesh		*spirit*
immanence		*transcendence*
what not to do	*what to do and be*	*what to be/not to be*

The essay is that form—perhaps *a*-generic, as Roland Barthes averred—wherein fiction and philosophy, experience and meaning, letter and spirit cross. When a novel shifts into the didactic or hortatory, it verges on the essay: Hermann Hesse's *Siddhartha*, for instance, in which experience serves mainly as a backdrop and occasion for analysis, reflection, and discrimination of meaning. Moreover, fiction's job, arguably, is not so much to show us how to live our lives but, instead, how *not* to live, what mistakes to (try to) avoid. Its way is very nearly the *via negativa*. Fiction, that is, shows us "how it is," rather than telling us how it ought to be (although hints and guesses are, of course, very often dropped or at least implied). Philosophy, on the other hand, concerns itself not with "how it is," not with experience as fiction represents it in all its particularity, its specificity, and its detail, as well as its muck and mire, thus with the very *texture* of living, but with what to be and not to be. Fiction roots itself in the material; philosophy houses in the transcendent world of ideas. As transcendent as fiction appears immanent, philosophy, we may say, treats disembodied ideas. Ideas that fiction represents are embodied in form, in characters, and events. Philosophy works on questions of being to the extent that fiction treats matters, ways, and results of doing.

Between fiction and philosophy, essays reflect, more or less directly, on what *to* do. They are more openly didactic and more often hortatory (see Thoreau, notably, and, differently, Bacon) than fiction. The essayist sometimes, as in the "hermit of Walden," launches admonitions from a soapbox, often prophetically declaims in the service of an implied program. More often than deserved, the essay has been linked to the sermon, itself ultimately positive even in the face of numerous and powerful "thou shalt not's." Like the sermon, in any case, the essay aspires to what drives philosophy: it aims to direct its readers not just toward what to do but also, thereby, how to *be*. I essay to be, declared Emerson, summarizing the way the ear steadfastly refuses to separate *essay* from *esse*. Being, for the essay, is always incarnate; that is, attainable only in, through, and by means of the "detour" that is our everyday life of doing.

THE ESSAY cannot save the world, despite the glory with which I seem to have enshrouded it. Nor is the essay by any means the greatest literary form or kind—only distinctive. It is less grand than fiction, more skeptical, including of itself, than philosophy. In its self-effacing, modest, and humble way, it does, however, point to Ultimate Truth. Georg Lukács may have mistaken the essay's *way* of approaching Truth, thinking direct, unmediated access was possible and so missing the necessary "detour" by means of which you reach transcendence only through immanence, but he recognized a certain undeniable character of essays when he described their maker as "a John the Baptist who goes out to preach in the wilderness about another who is still to come, whose shoelace he is not worthy to untie."[1]

EVEN SO, the essay tends to be stubbornly, although not stridently, secular, reflecting its Renaissance basis. Its realm, as we have seen, is that of individual man experiencing the concrete particulars of everyday life. You cannot remain long in the midst of essays and fail to appreciate Pope's account of the *via media* in *An Essay on Man*; indeed, the famous opening of that great poem's—and great essay's—second "epistle" reads like an account of the form Montaigne gave us in its mode, its manner, and its characteristic concerns, including, of course, the shared injunction to look into man and leave alone those matters that really are no concern to him in his everyday existence. I quote it again:

> Know then thyself, presume not God to scan;
> The proper study of Mankind is Man.
> Plac'd on this isthmus of a middle state,
> A being darkly wise, and rudely great:
> With too much knowledge for the Sceptic side,
> With too much weakness for the Stoic's pride,
> He hangs between; in doubt to act, or rest,
> In doubt to deem himself a God, or Beast;
> In doubt his Mind or Body to prefer,
> Born but to die, and reas'ning but to err;
> Alike in ignorance, his reason such,

> Whether he thinks too little, or too much:
> Chaos of Thought and Passion, all confus'd;
> Still by himself abus'd, or disabus'd;
> Created half to rise, and half to fall;
> Great lord of all things, yet a prey to all;
> Sole judge of Truth, in endless Error hurl'd:
> The glory, jest, and riddle of the world! (2.1–18)[2]

Modesty, born of clear-sighted awareness of man's capacities and incapacities, along with hard-bitten realism forbids ambitious and proud interference in realms other than this earthly one. That refusal need not, however, entail Godlessness or lack of faith.

I have said that the essay takes its particular coloration and texture and assumes its own place on the spectrum of forms in mining meaning from experience and assaying it. In so doing, I have suggested, the essay participates in that universal pattern we call Incarnation, the supreme instance of which is Christ's embodying of God, immanence and transcendence uniquely come together. The danger—and it is a "a signal and shattering one"—is that the premium the essay places on the Ordinary will turn into idolatry. I thus follow, up to a point, Cynthia Ozick in her brilliant essay "The Riddle of the Ordinary." Defining ordinariness "as a breathing-space: the breathing-space between getting born and dying, perhaps; or else the breathing-space between rapture and rupture; or, more usually, the breathing-space between one disaster and the next," Ozick insists that the Ordinary

> *does* deserve our gratitude. The Ordinary lets us live out our humanity; it doesn't scare us, it doesn't excite us, it doesn't distract us—it brings us the safe return of the school bus every day, it lets us eat

one meal after another, put one foot in front of the other. In short, it is equal to the earth's provisions; it grants us life, continuity, the leisure to recognize who and what we are, and who and what our fellows are, these creatures who live out their everydayness side by side with us in their own unextraordinary ways.[3]

The danger arises—and as a Jew, Ozick acknowledges that she is uncompromising and "stiff-necked"—because "if we are enjoined to live in the condition of noticing all things—or, to put it more extremely but more exactly, in the condition of awe—*how can we keep ourselves from sliding off from awe at God's Creation to worship of God's Creation?*" For Ozick, again as a Jew, to worship the creation would be idolatry, which she defines as that condition of allowing something—*anything*—to come between ourselves and God: "The Creator is not contained in his own Creation; the Creator is incarnate in nothing, and is free of any image or imagining."[4]

Here I part company with Ozick, subscribing as I do not only to incarnation but also to *the* Incarnation. Still, I find her question compelling. How do we get, she asks, from the Ordinary to the Extraordinary: if we are so concerned with the ordinary, that province the essay enjoins us to attend to and perhaps even to understand with awe, are we not locked into it and prevented from access to the Transcendent, the Extraordinary? In the pattern the essay enacts, I have claimed, meaning plays transcendent to experience's immanent, but that is only a structural participation in that pattern, shorn of its content—content that is religious and partakes of the Extraordinary.

To say, as apologists for the essay are wont to do, that this venerable form derives both its particularity and its significance from embrace of the Extraordinary *in* the Ordinary unfortunately resolves little. Ozick is alert to this move also and will have none of it: "The world, and every moment in it, is seen to be sublime, and not merely 'seen to be,' but brought home to the intensest part of consciousness." What this means, she offers as incontrovertible: "Saying 'Experience itself is the end' is the very opposite of blessing the Creator as the source of all experience."[5] What, though, for the Christian, who accepts—and is defined by that acceptance of—the doctrine of the Incarnation? The Extraordinary, to continue with Ozick's term, appears in the person of Jesus Christ, God become man. But that by no means commits us to the conclusion Ozick also rightly rejects: the Extraordinary appears in the Ordinary but is not equivalent to it, no more than meaning is identical to (mere) experience. There is an extra dimension to which experience, including experience of the Ordinary, gives us access. The trouble is, essays often do not (*pace* Lukács) reach for that dimension—exceptions include those of Annie Dillard, Wendell Berry, Peter Matthiessen, and Scott Sanders himself, notably in *The Force of Spirit*. Essays derive meaning, all right, but it is more often that meaning that remains on the level of the Ordinary and so does not attain that transcendent level, meaning that, in other words, does not transcend the Ordinary. Meaning is, in such an instance, etiolated and falls short of its potential—it is reduced.

As I say, exceptions occur, not only in earlier writing that we do not ordinarily think of as essays—for instance, the aforementioned *An Essay on Criticism* and *An Essay on Man*. Since these are in verse, we usually do not consider them as essays, despite their titles. Surely, however, with a writer as meticulous, fastidious, and fussy as Pope we should accord the benefit of any doubt. Moreover, these poems bear the marks of familiar essays: exploratory, experiential, "lay" in texture, un- (and even anti-) dogmatic, modest in approach, conversational in tone (and address), personal and brilliantly artful, deeply reflective and intensely moral, and celebratory of the *via media* (especially the later poem). These poems root themselves in the moral world: *Criticism* fully as much as *Man* insisting that the effective critic must, first of all, be a *vir bonus*. The concern of these poems is with man in his relations with "the world," with other men, and with himself.

But these poems do not exclude "the Ultimate," for if "the proper study of Mankind is Man," he nevertheless is measured, assayed, and judged as well by what shines through his everyday conduct. Through *this* world we are—or should be—led upward to God. At best, then, as Pope makes abundantly clear near the poem's end, "human soul/ Must rise from Individual to the Whole," and so he seeks to be one who,

> Slave to no sect, . . . takes no private road,
> But looks thro' Nature, up to Nature's God;
> Pursues that Chain which links th'immense Design,
> Joins heav'n and earth, and mortal and divine;
> Sees, that no being any bliss can know,
> But touches some above, and some below;
> Learns, from this union of the rising Whole,
> The first, last purpose of the human soul;
> And knows where Faith, Law, Morals, all began,
> All end, in LOVE of GOD, and LOVE of MAN. (4.331–40)

The way is *a posteriori*, moving (upward) from what we know (here below), unlike that manner of "reasoning downward" that Pope later attacks as cataclysmic in the fourth book of *The Dunciad*.

The unwary often blame Pope, branding him as Deistical or even atheistical—just as did at least one early reader of Dryden's *Religio Laici or A Laymans Faith*. This poem, too, is an essay, although Dryden did not so call it; still, it bears the marks of the familiar essay, even more than Pope's *Essays*. Indeed, *Religio Laici* embodies the range of the form's possibilities. It reveals how the essay can aspire to, reach, and reflect on ultimate concerns.

AS A LAYMAN'S FAITH, to begin with, Dryden's work shares the perspectives, interests, and values of the amateur, the common reader, and indeed the essayist, each of these four an analogue of the others—indeed here, the four come together more definitively than in any other place I know. Dryden thus represents man's ecclesiastical choice in moral terms, much like the later Pope—the preferred way here, however, is explicitly moderate, a holy compromise between competing extremes:

> What then remains, but, waving each Extreme,
> The Tides of Ignorance, and Pride to stem?
> Neither so rich a Treasure to forgo;
> Nor proudly seek beyond our pow'r to know: (427–30)[6]

Like Pope, Dryden would have the layman restrict himself to the realm of common concerns and sense, leaving abstruse theological questions to churchmen:

> If still our Reason runs another way,
> That private Reason 'tis more Just to curb,
> Than by Disputes the publick Peace disturb.
> For points obscure are of small use to learn:
> But *Common quiet* is *Mankind's concern*. (446–50)

The public thus takes precedence over the private, the individual needing to subordinate himself to the whole.

The issue is stubbornly moral: Dryden represents religious choices as reflective of the kind of person one is. Thus early on we read:

> Dar'st thou, poor Worm, offend *Infinity*?
> And must the Terms of Peace be given by *Thee*?
> Then *Thou* art *Justice* in the *last Appeal*;
> *Thy easie God* instructs Thee to *rebell*:
> And, like a King remote, and weak, must take
> What Satisfaction *Thou* art pleas'd to make. (93–98)

In addition to foregrounding the nature of the "layman," amateur, and common reader, Dryden's contribution, including to the essay, is this: he makes the issues at hand a matter of character, and then he draws out the political and religious implications of the moral stance one bodies forth.

And always it is a matter of embodiment, for the various religious and ecclesiastical positions are represented not in the abstract, as free-floating ideas and options, but instead in persons. People are everywhere here: the priest whose book *The Critical His-*

tory of the Old Testament, Dryden says, "occasion'd" his poem; the young translator of that tome to whom the poet addresses his work; the Deist, the Catholic, the sectarian; the directly addressed reader; and not least the poet-layman himself. The Deist reveals both pride and ignorance, as do differently the Papist and the despicable, lowly, and vile sectarian, who, in the face of the priesthood of all believers, turns this good into a worse consequence. The issue is clear: how one acts and conducts himself vis-à-vis Holy Scripture—the way of reading or responding to the text—is emblematic of the kind of person one is, be it proud, arrogant, and ignorant, or humble, balanced, and commonsensical. The matter is of ultimate concern, and the manner is a question of character:

> So all we make of Heavens discover'd Will
> Is, not to have it, or to use it ill.
> The Danger's much the same; on several Shelves
> If *others* wreck *us*, or *we* wreck our *selves*. (423–26)

The sectarian stands convicted, along with the Catholic and the Deist. Alone remains the poet, modestly inquiring, "what then remains, but, waving each Extreme" somehow to stem "The Tides of Ignorance, and Pride" (427–28). It would not be quite accurate to conclude that *Religio Laici* reveals how one's religious position itself shows what kind of person he is. For while that is true, according to the poem, character is the field on which warring forces contend. Character is, in fact, the basis of the poem, the ground of the discussion of public, political, and religious questions of the greatest import. Your way of approaching and treating God's Holy Word reveals your character, shows who and what you are as a person. As in all essays, the issue of character constitutes the starting point.

The desired alternative to the competing extremes of pride and ignorance appears only in the poem's speaker, a model of common sense, public concern, and humility. He is a layman who gratefully accepts the Reformation's gift, a freedom of access to Scripture that he uses responsibly. The *via media*, which, ecclesiastically, is only the Church of England, appears in the poem as represented by and embodied in the poet: he *is* the poem's embodied truth.

In *Religio Laici*, character reveals all, holding nothing in reserve—and pointing the way open to the essay. Here the poem shows the way, opening the essay up to the ultimate, religious implications of character. As I have been suggesting, *Religio Laici* is not about doctrine, acceptance of doctrine, or even ecclesiastical position so much as it is about pride and ignorance and what they portend when we extend consideration to "ultimate" issues.

From the beginning, *Religio Laici* acts in accordance with what Dryden writes in the justly admired exordium:

> DIM, as the borrow'd beams of Moon and Stars
> To *lonely, weary, wandring* Travellers,
> Is *Reason* to the *Soul*: And as on high,
> Those rowling Fires *discover* but the Sky
> Not light us *here*; So *Reason*'s glimmering Ray
> Was lent, not to *assure* our *doubtfull* way,
> But *guide* us upward to a *better Day*. (1–7)

The marked triplet is Dryden's way of signaling the importance of this last idea, an indication, it turns out, of his poem's "immanent form." For *Religio Laici* does precisely what he writes here: in movement and message, it guides us upward to God and away from the self's interested machinations and usurped authority. That idea governs direction, for even the layman's faith—a not-insignificant minor tradition that includes works by Sir Thomas Browne and Lord Herbert of Cherbury—proves of little effect.

In the various respects I have noted—including "immanent form," "embodied truth," moral focus, and ultimate concern—*Religio Laici* appears an exemplary, a consummate essay (although, I shall argue elsewhere, T. S. Eliot's *Four Quartets* moves even closer to that midpoint between experience and meaning, poetry and philosophy). Little else I know matches this paradigmatic essay that in its modesty does not even claim the term.

NOTES

Introduction

1. I have elaborated on these themes in "Envisioning the Stranger's Heart," *College English* 56 (1994): 629–41. The title of this piece I borrow from Cynthia Ozick's "Metaphor and Memory," included in her collection of that name (New York: Knopf, 1989).
2. Douglas Bauer, "The Pack Mule of Prose: Thoughts on the Sentence," *Writer's Chronicle* 36 (September 2003): 40–46.
3. Thomas Harrison, *Essayism* (Baltimore: Johns Hopkins University Press, 1992).
4. Jonathan Swift, *A Tale of a Tub*, in *"Gulliver's Travels" and Other Writings*, ed. Louis A. Landa (Boston: Riverside-Houghton Mifflin, 1960), 352.
5. *Antioch Review* 51.4 (Fall 1993).

Irony or Sneakiness: On the Essay's Second-Class Citizenship

1. Georg Lukács, "On the Nature and Form of the Essay," in *Soul and Form*, trans. Anna Bostock (Cambridge: MIT Press, 1974), 9.
2. Michel de Montaigne, *The Complete Essays*, trans. Donald M. Frame (Stanford: Stanford University Press, 1958), 272–73.
3. Ibid., 273.
4. Ibid., 274.
5. Ibid., 275.
6. Abraham Cowley, "Of Greatness," in *Essays*, 1678 (London, 1886), 120.
7. T. S. Eliot, *A Sermon* (Cambridge: Cambridge University Press, 1948), 7.

8. T. S. Eliot, *Charles Whibley: A Memoir*. English Association Pamphlet No. 80 (December, 1931): 12.

9. Phillip Lopate, ed., *The Art of the Personal Essay* (New York: Anchor-Doubleday, 1994), xxxii.

10. Richard Selzer, "An Absence of Windows," in *The Art of the Essay*, ed. Lydia Fakundiny (Boston: Houghton Mifflin, 1991), 434.

11. Samuel Johnson, quoted in Virginia Woolf, *The Common Reader* (New York: Harcourt, Brace, 1925), 11–12.

12. Woolf, *The Common Reader*, 11–12.

13. Clara Claiborne Park, *Rejoining the Common Reader* (Evanston: Northwestern University Press, 1991), 5, 13.

14. Cynthia Ozick, "The Riddle of the Ordinary," in *The Art of the Essay*, 421.

15. Ibid.

16. Lukács, "On the Nature and Form," 9.

17. Ibid.

18. Ibid., 9–10.

19. Hilaire Belloc, "The Mowing of a Field," in *Hills and the Sea*, 1906 (Marlboro, VT: Marlboro Press, n.d.), 147.

20. Ibid., 148.

Home-Cosmography: The Renaissance Basis of the Essay

1. Michel de Montaigne, *The Complete Essays*, trans. Donald M. Frame (Stanford: Stanford University Press, 1958), 272–73.

2. William Cornwallis, cited in *The Art of the Essay*, ed. Lydia Fakundiny (Boston: Houghton Mifflin, 1991), 13.

3. Montaigne, *The Complete Essays*, 273.

4. Ibid., 274.

5. Philip P. Hallie, *The Scar of Montaigne: An Essay in Personal Philosophy* (Middletown, CT: Wesleyan University Press, 1966), 9–10.

6. W. Wolfgang Holdheim, "Introduction: The Essay as Knowledge in Progress," in *The Hermeneutic Mode: Essays on Time in Literature and Literary Theory* (Ithaca: Cornell University Press, 1984).

7. Hallie, *The Scar of Montaigne*, 13.

8. Ibid., 14.

9. Montaigne, "Of the Art of Discussion," quoted in Hallie, *The Scar of Montaigne*, 15.

10. Hallie, *The Scar of Montaigne*, 21.

11. Montaigne, quoted in Fakundiny, *The Art of the Essay*, 678.

12. Emerson, quoted in William H. Gass, "Emerson and the Essay," in *Habitations of the Word* (New York: Simon and Schuster, 1985), 15.

13. John Dryden, *Religio Laici or A Laymans Faith* (1682), in *Poems and Fables*, ed. James Kinsley (Oxford: Oxford University Press, 1962).

14. Virginia Woolf, "How Should One Read a Book?," in *The Common Reader: Second Series* (London: Hogarth Press, 1932), 258.

15. Ibid.

16. Ibid., 270.

17. Gass, "Emerson and the Essay," 25.

18. Walter Pater, in *The Renaissance*, quoted in Graham Good, *The Observing Self: Rediscovering the Essay* (London: Routledge, 1988), 45.

19. Good, *The Observing Self*, 45.

20. Edward Hoagland, "What I Think, What I Am," in Fakundiny, *The Art of the Essay*, 691.

21. Good, *The Observing Self*, 47.

The Most Self-Centered of Forms? Distinguishing the Essay

1. Michel de Montaigne, "Of Practice," in *The Complete Essays*, trans. Donald M. Frame (Stanford: Stanford University Press, 1958), 273–74.

2. Henry David Thoreau, *Walden*, 1854 (New York: Library of America, 1991), 5.

3. Lawrence Buell, *The Environmental Imagination: Thoreau, Nature Writing, and the Formation of American Culture* (Cambridge: Belknap-Harvard University Press, 1995).

4. Scott Russell Sanders, "The Singular First Person," in *Secrets of the Universe: Scenes from the Journey Home* (Boston: Beacon Press, 1991).

5. Jonathan Swift, *The Battle of the Books*, 1704, in *"Gulliver's Travels" and Other Writings*, ed. Louis A. Landa (Boston: Riverside-Houghton Mifflin, 1960), 368, 367.

6. William H. Gass, "Emerson and the Essay," in *Habitations of the Word* (New York: Simon and Schuster, 1985), 26–27.

7. Phillip Lopate, ed., *The Art of the Personal Essay* (New York: Anchor-Doubleday, 1994), xxvii.

8. Nancy Mairs, "On Being a Cripple," in *Plaintext* (Tucson: University of Arizona Press, 1986), 20.

9. Zora Neale Hurston, "How It Feels to Be Colored Me," in *The Art of the Essay*, ed. Lydia Fakundiny (Boston: Houghton Mifflin, 1991), 294.

10. Ibid.

11. Richard Selzer, "A Worm from My Notebook," in Fakundiny, *The Art of the Essay*, 434.

12. Lopate, *The Art of the Personal Essay*, xxviii.

13. Theodor Adorno, "The Essay as Form," quoted in Lopate, *The Art of the Personal Essay*, xliii.

14. Buell, *The Environmental Imagination*, 177.

15. Ibid., 122.

16. Ibid., 178–179.

17. William Wordsworth, *The Prelude*, in *Selected Poems and Prefaces*, ed. Jack Stillinger (Boston: Riverside-Houghton Mifflin, 1965), 366.

18. Hilaire Belloc, "The Mowing of a Field," in *Hills and the Sea*, 1906 (Marlboro, VT: Marlboro Press, n.d.), 147, 149–50.

19. Ibid., 151, 149.

20. Lopate, *The Art of the Personal Essay*, xxxii.

Assaying Experience: Time, Meaning, and the Essay

1. George Core, "Stretching the Limits of the Essay," in *Essays on the Essay: Redefining the Genre*, ed. Alexander J. Butrym (Athens: University of Georgia Press, 1989), 217.
2. Scott Russell Sanders, "The Singular First Person," in *Secrets of the Universe: Scenes from the Journey Home* (Boston: Beacon Press, 1991), 189.
3. Ibid., 189–90.
4. William Wordsworth, "Preface to *Lyrical Ballads*," in *Selected Poems and Prefaces*, ed. Jack Stillinger (Boston: Riverside-Houghton Mifflin, 1965), 446–49.
5. Richard Selzer, "A Worm from My Notebook," in *The Art of the Essay*, ed. Lydia Fakundiny (Boston: Houghton Mifflin, 1991), 434.
6. Alexander Smith, *Dreamthorp* (London, 1863).
7. John Keats, *Selected Poems and Letters*, ed. Douglas Bush (Boston: Riverside-Houghton Mifflin, 1959), 279, 263.
8. Anne Carson, interview by Mary Gannon, *Poets & Writers Magazine*, 29 (March-April 2001), 33.
9. Wordsworth, "Preface to *Lyrical Ballads*," 448–49.
10. Henry David Thoreau, *Walden*, 1854 (New York: Library of America, 1991), 34, 18.
11. Ibid., 74–75.
12. Ibid., 79, 75.
13. E. B. White, "A Slight Sound at Evening," in *Essays* (New York: Harper and Row, 1977), 236, 235, 238.
14. Ibid., 241.
15. Sanders, "Speaking a Word for Nature," in *Secrets of the Universe*, 221–222.
16. Ibid., 223.
17. Ibid., 226.

18. Edward Hoagland, "What I Think, What I Am," in Fakundiny, *The Art of the Essay*, 691.

19. Ezra Pound, trans., *The Great Digest and Unwobbling Pivot* (New York: New Directions, 1951), 27–29.

20. Michel de Montaigne, *The Complete Essays*, trans. Donald M. Frame (Stanford: Stanford University Press, 1958), 300: "Seneca more undulating and diverse."

21. Samuel F. Pickering, Jr., "Composing a Life," in *A Continuing Education* (Hanover, NH: University Press of New England, 1985), 157–58.

22. Selzer, "A Worm from My Notebook," 434–35.

23. Keats, *Selected Poems and Letters*, 279.

24. Ibid., 263.

25. Montaigne, "On Experience," 850–51.

26. Roland Barthes, "An Almost Obsessive Relation to Writing Instruments," in *The Grain of the Voice: Interviews 1962–1980*, trans. Linda Coverdale, 1985 (Berkeley: University of California Press, 1991), 178.

27. Edmund White, in *The Writer's Desk*, ed. Jill Krementz (New York: Random House, 1996), 108.

28. G. Douglas Atkins, "On Writing Well: Or, Springing the Genie from the Inkpot," *JAC*, 20 (2000), 73–85. See also my follow-up essay, "Art and Anger—Upon Taking Up the Pen Again: Self(e)-Expression," *JAC*, 20 (2000), 414–26.

29. Barthes, "An Almost Obsessive Relation," 177–178.

30. Hilaire Belloc, "The Mowing of a Field," in *Hills and the Sea*, 1906 (Marlboro, VT: Marlboro Press, n.d.), 148.

31. Ezra Pound, *ABC of Reading*, 1934 (New York: New Directions, 1960), 28.

32. Cynthia Ozick, "The Seam of the Snail," in *Metaphor and Memory* (New York: Knopf, 1989), 109–10.

Paradox Abounding: Tension and the Via Media Nature of the Essay

1. T. S. Eliot, *The Dry Salvages*, in *Four Quartets* (New York: Harcourt, Brace, 1943).

2. John Dryden, *Religio Laici or A Laymans Faith*, in *Poems and Fables*, ed. James Kinsley (Oxford: Oxford University Press, 1962).

3. Edward Hoagland, "What I Think, What I Am," in *The Art of the Essay*, ed. Lydia Fakundiny (Boston: Houghton Mifflin, 1991), 692.

4. Scott Russell Sanders, "The Singular First Person," in *Secrets of the Universe: Scenes from the Journey Home* (Boston: Beacon Press, 1991), 189–90.

5. Henry David Thoreau, *Walden*, 1854 (New York: Library of America, 1991), 5, 257.

6. Ralph Waldo Emerson, quoted in William H. Gass, "Emerson and the Essay," in *Habitations of the Word* (New York: Simon and Schuster, 1985), 15.

7. Phillip Lopate, ed., *The Art of the Personal Essay* (New York: Anchor-Doubleday, 1994), xliv.

8. T. S. Eliot, *Essays Ancient and Modern* (London: Faber and Faber, 1936), 148–49.

9. Ibid., 146, 150–51.

10. Alexander Pope, *Poetry and Prose*, ed. Aubrey Williams (Boston: Riverside-Houghton-Mifflin, 1969).

11. Sanders, "The Singular First Person," 190–91.

12. Michel de Montaigne, "Of Practice," in *The Complete Essays*, trans. Donald M. Frame (Stanford: Stanford University Press, 1958), 272.

13. Jeanette Winterson, *Art Objects: Essays on Ecstasy and Effrontery* (New York: Knopf, 1996), 184–185.

14. T. S. Eliot, "Tradition and the Individual Talent," in *The Sacred Wood* (London, Methuen, 1920), 45.

15. Ibid., 44–45.

16. G. Douglas Atkins, "In Other Words: Gardening for Love—The Work of the Essayist," *Kenyon Review*, ns 13 (1991), 56–69.

17. Tom Paulin, *Writing to the Moment: Selected Critical Essays* (London: Faber and Faber, 1996), xi.

18. Ibid.

19. Geoffrey H. Hartman, *Criticism in the Wilderness* (New Haven: Yale University Press, 1980), 49–50.

20. Georg Lukács, "On the Nature and Form of the Essay," in *Soul and Form*, trans. Ann Bostock (Cambridge: MIT Press, 1974), 9.

21. Fakundiny, *The Art of the Essay*, 678.

22. Eliot, "Tradition and the Individual Talent," 52–53.

23. T. S. Eliot, *A Sermon* (Cambridge: Cambridge University Press, 1948), 7.

24. Eliot, "Tradition and the Individual Talent," 53.

25. G. K. Chesterton, "A Piece of Chalk," in Lopate, *The Art of the Personal Essay*, 252.

26. Ibid., 251, 250.

27. Robert Browning, "Fra Lippo Lippi," in *Robert Browning's Poetry*, ed. James F. Loucks (New York: Norton, 1979).

Form and Meaning: The Essay's Immanent Purposiveness

1. Edward Hoagland, "What I Think, What I Am," in *The Art of the Essay*, ed. Lydia Fakundiny (Boston: Houghton Mifflin, 1991), 691, and Joseph Epstein, "Piece Work: Writing the Essay," in *Plausible Prejudices: Essays on American Writing* (New York: Norton, 1985), 400.

2. Scott Russell Sanders, "Under the Influence," *Secrets of the Universe: Scenes from the Journey Home* (Boston: Beacon Press, 1991), 6–7.

3. Hoagland, "What I Think, What I Am," 692.

4. Jeanette Winterson, *Art Objects: Essays on Ecstasy and Effrontery* (New York: Knopf, 1996), 105–6.

5. Sanders, "Under the Influence," 5–6.

6. Ibid., 21–22.

7. William H. Gass, "Emerson and the Essay," in *Habitations of the Word* (New York: Simon and Schuster, 1985), 25.

8. Sanders, "Under the Influence," 22.

9. Ibid.

10. Ibid., 23.

11. E. B. White, "Death of a Pig," *Essays* (New York: Harper and Row, 1977), 17.

12. Ibid., 17–18.

13. Ibid., 18–19.

14. Ibid., 20–21.

15. Ibid., 22.

16. Ibid., 24.

17. Hilaire Belloc, "The Mowing of a Field," in *Hills and the Sea*, 1906 (Marlboro, VT: Marlboro Press, n.d.), 146.

18. Ibid., 147.

19. Ibid., 149–50.

20. Ibid., 150–51.

In-Betweenness: The Burden of the Essay

1. Georg Lukács, "On the Nature and Form of the Essay," in *Soul and Form*, trans. Anna Bostock (Cambridge: MIT Press, 1974), 16.

2. Alexander Pope, *Poetry and Prose*, ed. Aubrey Williams (Boston: Riverside-Houghton Mifflin, 1969).

3. Cynthia Ozick, "The Riddle of the Ordinary," in *The Art of the Essay*, ed. Lydia Fakundiny (Boston: Houghton Mifflin, 1991), 417, 416–17.

4. Ibid., 421.

5. Ibid., 420–21.

6. John Dryden, *Religio Laici or A Laymans Faith*, in *Poems and Fables*, ed. James Kinsley (Oxford: Oxford University Press, 1962).

INDEX

Adorno, Theodor, 25, 55, 129

amateur. *See* common reader; essayist: as amateur; layman's faiths

antidogmatism, of essays, 4–5, 15, 55, 119, 157

Antioch Review, 6

Aristotle, 136

Arnold, Matthew, 58, 70, 107–8

article, vs. essay, 3–4, 11, 41–42, 44, 56, 67, 81, 92, 117–18, 132, 147

art of living, 32–34, 66, 75, 88–89

assaying: essay as, 51, 65–94 passim, 108, 117, 148, 154

author, vs. speaker, 133–44 passim, 148

authority, individual, 41, 111, 117–18

autobiography, vs. essay, 3, 68–69, 100, 151

Bacon, Francis, 1–2, 29, 31, 57–58, 101, 152; as different from Montaigne, 42–44, 56, 61, 105–6, 108–9, 112, 118

balance: and composition, 83, 91; and tension, 54, 58. *See also* composition; composure

Barthes, Roland, 89–90; essay described as *a*-generic by, 151

being, and the essay, 34, 102, 115, 152

Belloc, Hilaire, 1–2, 16, 89–91, 116; cultural critique by, 60; as different from Wordsworth, 59–60; and pens, 89. Work: "Mowing of a Field, The," 6, 22–24, 58–60, 79, 140–44

Berry, Wendell, 150, 156

Browne, Sir Thomas, 3, 162

Browning, Robert, 55; "Fra Lippo Lippi," 121–22. *See also* incarnation

Buell, Lawrence, 49, 56–57

Burns, Robert, 71

Byron, George Gordon, Lord, 80

Carlyle, Thomas: *Sartor Resartus*, 150

Carroll, Lewis, 58

Carson, Anne: on essay as reflection, 71, 81–82

character, 4, 83, 88, 161

Chesterton, G. K., 116; "Piece of Chalk, A," 6, 24–25, 120–22, 144

Christianity, 15–16, 19, 86, 120–21

Coleridge, Samuel Taylor, 67, 70, 86, 147
common reader: essayist as, 17–18, 38–42, 158–59
composition, 128; of character, 88–89, 91; meanings of, 83
composure, 53–54, 91. *See also* balance
Confucius, 55, 82–83, 86
Cornwallis, Sir William, 29–31
Cowley, Abraham: "Of Greatness," 15
Critical History of the Old Testament, The, 159–60
criticism, and essay, 11, 21, 113
culture of self-esteem, 61, 97–99, 101

Dante Alighieri, 34, 99
Davis, Walter A., 125–26, 128
Derrida, Jacques, 45, 113
Didion, Joan, 83, 108; "On Morality," 116
Dillard, Annie, 100, 128, 156
discontent, and the essay, 12
disembodiment, 126, 152; in Chesterton, 120. *See also* embodied truth; incarnation
Donne, John, 29
Dryden, John, 41–42, 113; and Eliot, 111. Works: *Hind and the Panther, The*, 122; *Religio Laici*, 35–40, 44, 98, 111, 117, 158–61

ego, 16, 49
Eliot, T. S., 2, 7, 50, 70, 99, 106–7; as against the thoroughgoing, 111; and autobiography, 110; and Dryden, 111; and Hartman, 113–14; and the impersonal, 50, 87–88, 109, 117; and incarnation, 150; on Montaigne and Pascal, 103–4; and personality, 108–10; and Whibley, 15–18; against Wordsworth, 117. Works: *Four Quartets*, 98, 162; *Sermon, A*, 120; "Tradition and the Individual Talent," 109–11, 117–18
embodied truth, 125, 159, 161; essay as, 5, 133–44 passim, 147, 162. *See also* disembodiment; incarnation
Emerson, Ralph Waldo, 65, 116; and essaying to be, 34, 80, 102, 152
enthusiasm: religious, 97, 112–13
Epictetus, 66
Epstein, Joseph, 6, 61, 116, 127
Erasmus, 32–33
essay: alleged death of, 65, 100; alleged irony of, 20–22, 24, 119; as artistic structure, 43; as critique, 12, 22, 66, 78, 107–8; as crucible, 6, 50–51, 81, 116; effects

of, 3–5, 7, 32–33; historical changes in [history of *or* changes in], 58–59, 61; indirectness in, 11–25 passim, 60, 66, 114, 121–22, 150–52; as inductive, 107–8, 112, 116, 150, 157–58; lessons of, 79; literal nature of, 5, 24, 150; modest manner of, 6, 11–25 passim, 52, 119–20, 152, 154, 157, 162; as new form, 13, 29–31, 34; openness of, 4, 81, 91, 107; as personal and artful, 2, 119, 157; point of, 81, 116; predecessors of, 29; and the present, 141; as reflective, 71, 82, 101, 117, 129, 148–50, 152, 157; renaissance of, 11, 100; as rooted, 83–84, 119; as second-class citizen, 11, 20–21, 25, 69; as secular, 153; as self-centered, 14, 49–61 passim, 78, 88, 101, 108; and sentences, 1–3, 88; and shape, 133; structure of, as incarnation, 69, 119; subject of, 6, 52, 68, 84–85, 116–17, 141, 148–49; teachings of, 2–4, 12, 43, 79, 82, 85, 98, 108–9 (*see also* slowing down); as trial or attempt, 2, 12, 29, 56, 71, 75, 81; will of, 6, 73, 101, 106; as witness, 78; writing of, 1–4, 6, 82, 85

essayism, 5

essayist: as amateur, 41–42, 54, 65, 158–59; as common reader, 17–18, 38–42, 158–59; as layman, 41–42, 54, 157–59, 161–62; individuality of, 16, 100, 116; literal imagination of, 150

essayistic: character, 20, 41; spirit, 114–15; teaching, 4, 43

esse, 152

experience, individual, 33–34, 65–66, 107; value of, 34, 43, 108

Fakundiny, Lydia, 88, 100, 114–15, 119, 148

familiar (essay), 71, 113, 118, 148; as different from personal (essay), 43, 60, 100–101, 116–17, 157

fiction, vs. essay, 148–52

Flaubert, Gustave: *Madame Bovary*, 7

form, 125–44 passim; as immanent, 68, 125–33 passim, 139, 151–55; as incarnate, 147; as in-dwelling, 127; as transcendent, 5. *See also* tension: as marking essay's form

Foucault, Michel, 98

Gass, William H., 41–42, 44, 51–52, 147

Good, Graham, 43

Harrison, Thomas: *Essayism*, 5

Hartman, Geoffrey H., 3, 20, 116; and Eliot, 113–14
Hazlitt, William, 2, 51, 58, 70, 112; "On Going a Journey," 44, 59, 129
Herbert, Edward, Lord of Cherbury, 162
Hesse, Hermann: *Siddhartha*, 151
Hoagland, Edward, 1, 44, 81, 100, 116, 129; "What I Think, What I Am," 101
home-cosmography, 34, 102, 105. *See also* mapping
Homer, 34, 99, 110
Humanism, 32
humility, as virtue of the essay, 4, 25, 52, 106, 152
Hurston, Zora Neale: "How It Feels to Be Colored Me," 53–54

Idler, 127
immanence, 5, 25, 68, 94, 126–28, 139; and transcendence, 31, 151–55. *See also* form: as immanent
immanent purposiveness, 125–44 passim. *See also* form; immanence; purposive movement
in-betweenness, of the essay, 44, 56, 105, 112, 114, 117, 119, 122, 147–62 passim

incarnation, 5, 85, 88, 105, 118, 144, 147, 150, 154–56; in "Fra Lippo Lippi," 121–22; structure of essay as, 69, 119. *See also* embodied truth; form
Incarnation, the, 155–56
individualism, 32, 38, 97, 109; of the essay, 45, 67, 101, 106, 109, 111. *See also* essayist
irony, 11–25 passim, 119. *See also* Lukács, Georg

Jeffrey, Francis, 113
Johnson, Samuel, 2, 17–18, 58, 100, 108

Keats, John, 70, 86–88, 90, 93
Kenko, 29, 108
Klee, Paul, 6, 73, 90. *See also* line
Krutch, Joseph Wood, 65

Lamb, Charles, 51, 58
layman's faiths, 35–38, 158–62. *See also* Dryden, John; essayist: as layman
letter and spirit in essay, 115, 119–22
line: "out for a walk," 6, 31, 73, 86, 90, 92, 94
littleness, essay's taste for, 15, 17, 21, 55, 120
living, art of, 32–34, 66, 75, 88–89

INDEX

Lopate, Phillip, 17, 52, 55, 100, 102, 116, 128

Lukàcs, Georg, 5–6, 12, 24–25, 114–15, 119–20, 152–53, 156; "On the Nature and Form of the Essay," 20–22

Luther, Martin 35

lyric, the, and essays, 70–71, 92, 147

Mairs, Nancy, 1, 116; "On Being a Cripple," 52–53

mapping: of the self, 13, 29–45 passim, 68, 101–2, 104. *See also* home-cosmography

Mason, Bobbie Ann, 76–77

McPhee, John, 50

meaning, 25; essay's extraction of, 6, 31, 68–69, 81, 116, 154, 156; intersection of, with experience, 5, 44–45, 70, 147–51, 162

"me" culture. *See* self-esteem, culture of

memoir, and the essay, 56, 61, 99–101, 116, 151

mindfulness (Zen), 90–91

Montaigne, Michel de, 2, 17, 25, 52, 55, 60, 66, 70, 114, 147; and Bacon, 42–44, 56, 57–58, 61, 105–6, 108–9, 112, 118; on composing, 83; deconstruction by, 32; Eliot on, 103–4; as father of the essay, 44; and Pope, 33–34, 88, 104–6, 153; and the self, 49, 101–2; writings of, as essays, 21. Works: "Of Books," 43; "Of Practice," 12–15, 29–31, 51, 69; "Of Solitude," 43

mood, and the essay, 70

nature, and the essay, 76–77

negative capability, 93

nonfiction, essay as, 115

novel, and essay, 147–49, 151

ordinary, the, 18–20, 67–68, 76, 150, 154–56

Orwell, George, 2, 58, 65, 107; *Animal Farm*, 134; "Shooting an Elephant," 116

Ozick, Cynthia, 1, 3, 20, 70–71, 87–88, 100; as against Christianity, 19, 154–55. Works: "Drugstore in Winter, A," 19; "Riddle of the Ordinary, The," 18–19, 86, 154–56; "Seam of the Snail, The," 19, 94

Park, Clara Claiborne, 18

particular, the, 51, 81–82, 84, 100, 107–8, 150, 153

Pascal, Blaise, 103–4

Pater, Walter, 43, 114

Paulin, Tom, 112–13
personal (essay), 43, 60, 100–101, 113, 116–17, 129, 157. *See also* familiar (essay)
personal, the, 7
personality, in essays, 117–18
philosophy, and essays, 102, 148–52
Pickering, Samuel F., Jr., 16–17, 50, 55, 89, 100, 115; "Composing a Life," 3, 83, 88
Plato, 150
Plutarch, 13, 29, 108
Pope, Alexander, 32, 73, 75, 80, 98–99, 147; and Montaigne, 33–34, 88, 104–6, 153. Works: *Essay on Criticism, An*, 88, 104, 156–58; *Essay on Man, An*, 104–5, 153–54, 156–58. *See also* Montaigne, Michel de
Pound, Ezra, 55, 73, 82–83, 92, 106–7, 109
process, 31; and product in writing, 43–45, 81. *See also* writing
product. *See* process
professional, the, purposive movement: in texts, 68, 125–29, 139. *See also* immanent purposiveness
Pyrrhonism, 103, 105

quotation in essays, 51–52

reader, essay's assumption of, 51
reading, 73–74, 76–77, 113, 160; effects of Reformation on, 35–36; and the Renaissance, 34; and writing, 2–3. *See also* Dryden, John; layman's faiths; Woolf, Virginia
Reformation, 35–36, 97, 108, 112, 161. *See also* individualism; layman's faiths; reading
Renaissance, 29–45 passim, 59, 97, 142, 153; essay as product of, 31, 68
Romanticism, essay and, 70, 86–87, 112–13, 120
Rousseau, Jean-Jacques, 98

Sanders, Scott Russell, 16, 50, 71, 101, 111; *Force of Spirit, The*, 156; "Singular First Person, The," 65, 76, 84, 106–7; "Speaking a Word for Nature," 76–78; "Under the Influence," 128–34, 139
self, as medium in essays, 116
self-correction, 55, 82–83, 99, 105–6
self-criticism, 22, 99
self-esteem, culture of, 61, 97–99, 101
self-expression, vs. essay, 129, 131
self-knowledge, quest for, 30, 86, 99, 101–2, 105–6, 132, 153

Selzer, Richard, 1, 3, 68, 71, 86, 100; "Absence of Windows, An," 17, 20, 54; "Worm from My Notebook, A," 54, 84–85, 149
Seneca, 12, 29, 83, 108
sermon, vs. essay, 120, 152
Shonagon, Sei, 29, 108
short story, vs. essay, 84, 148–49
simplicity, 73–76
skepticism, 5, 32, 69, 103–5; in essays, 5, 15, 104–5. *See also* Montaigne, Michel de
slowing down, 67, 69, 73, 79–82, 89–92, 140
Smith, Alexander: *Dreamthorp*, 70
speaker vs. author, 133–44 passim, 148
Spectator, 127, 147
spirit and letter in essay, 115, 119–22
Stevenson, Robert Louis, 55
Strunk, Will: *Elements of Style*, 89
Swift, Jonathan, 22, 80, 86, 98; *Battle of the Books, The*, 51; "Modest Proposal, A," 119, 144, 148; *Tale of a Tub, A*, 6, 51, 113
sympathetic: imagination, 86; understanding, 52

Tatler, 127, 147
Taylor, William, 113
tension, 20–21, 30, 54, 57–58, 107, 109, 117–19, 122, 134, 139; evolution of, in essays, 56, 58; as marking essay's form, 15–16, 31, 44–45, 56, 65, 111–12, 114, 142, 147. *See also via media*
Thoreau, Henry David, 16, 50, 65, 70, 76, 79–80, 89, 152; movement toward balance in works of, 49, 56–57. Works: *Walden*, 49, 56–58, 73–75; "Walking," 73, 116
time, 65–94 passim, 134; essay's respect for, 67; as subject of essay, 141; and timelessness, 69–70. *See also under* writing
transcendence, 93–94, 144, 151–55; and immanence, 31, 151–55

Ultimate, the, 21–22, 152, 157, 160–62

verse, essays in, 156–62 passim
via media, 44–45, 97–122 passim, 147, 153, 157, 161. *See also* tension
voice, 100, 111, 116, 129, 133, 147–48. *See also* essayist

Walton, Izaak: *Compleat Angler*, 106
Whibley, Charles, 16–17
White, Edmund, 89
White, Elwyn Brooks (E. B.), 2, 16, 54, 58, 65–66, 70, 79, 89; on

White, Elwyn Brooks (*continued*)
essay's basic ingredient, 4, 83; and essay's second-class citizenship, 11, 21, 25, 69; and essay's self-centeredness, 49–50, 52, 69, 88, 101, 108; and time, 69, 75–76, 141. Works: "Coon Tree," 69, 78; "Death of a Pig," 22, 55, 69, 116, 133–39, 141, 143; *Elements of Style*, 25, 89; "Once More to the Lake," 69, 141; "Report in January, A," 78; "Ring of Time, The," 69, 116, 141; "Slight Sound at Evening, A," 49, 75–76; "What Do Our Hearts Treasure?," 69, 141; "Winter of the Great Snows, The," 78

will: reading as battle of, 38; of writing, 6, 92

Winterson, Jeanette, 109, 118; on constitutiveness of form, 129

Woolf, Virginia, 2, 42, 58, 65, 108, 129, 148; *Common Reader, The*, 17–18; "Death of the Moth," 6, 116; "How Should One Read a Book?," 39–41; "On Being Ill," 3

Wordsworth, William, 60, 68, 71, 73, 76–77, 79, 87–88, 113, 117; poems of, as short essays, 58, 67, 70, 147–48. Works: *Lyrical Ballads*, Preface, 58, 66–67, 72, 97, 109; *Prelude, The*, 59, 86, 97; "Resolution and Independence," 58. *See also* Belloc, Hilaire

writing: and ceremony, 89–90, 93–94; and mindfulness, 90–91; pens and the art of, 89–90, 92–93; as process, 81, 91, 93, 114, 139; time required for, 80–81; and transcendence of egotism, 87; and value of workshops, 2. *See also* reading

Zen mindfulness, 90–91

www.ingramcontent.com/pod-product-compliance
Lightning Source LLC
Chambersburg PA
CBHW011751220426
43671CB00017B/2946